Webhooks

Events for RESTful APIs

Matthias Biehl

First edition: December 2017

Biehl, Matthias
    API-University Press
    Volume 4 of the API-University Series.
    Includes illustrations, bibliographical references and index.
    ISBN-13: 978-1979717069
    ISBN-10: 1979717060

API-University Press
http://www.api-university.com
info@api-university.com

Contents

Abstract

Got RESTful APIs? Great. API consumers love them. But today, such RESTful APIs are not enough for the evolving expectations of API consumers. Their apps need to be responsive, event-based and react to changes in near real-time.

This results in a new set of requirements for the APIs, which power the apps. APIs now need to provide concepts such as events, notifications, triggers, and subscriptions. These concepts are not natively supported by the REST architectural style.

The good thing: we can engineer RESTful APIs that support events with a webhook infrastructure. The bad thing: it requires some heavy lifting. The webhook infrastructure needs to be developer-friendly, easy to use, reliable, secure and highly available.

With the best practices and design templates provided in this book, we want to help you extend your API portfolio with a modern webhook infrastructure. So you can offer both APIs and events that developers love to use.

1 Introduction

Integration used to be all about APIs. Now it is about APIs and events. In this chapter, we explore why the demands for integration changed and how you can profit from the change.

1.1 Integration with APIs

APIs started out as a way to access data or call some function on a server. The pattern for integration with API was always: provide APIs and plug them together. With the right API, an application can simply call the API to get some specialized work done, e.g., to handle credit card payments or to send a bunch of SMS reminders to customers.

If we call an API, we expect it to deliver a response pretty much immediately. And so APIs deliver synchronous responses. However, the API should also tell us if one of those credit card payments did not go through, or when three of those SMS could not be delivered to the recipients. How? The API synchronously sends an error response. This works well if the calculation of the response does not require a long-running process.

But our examples, payment confirmation and SMS delivery confirmation, do require long-running processes. Thus responses cannot be returned synchronously. How then? Are APIs enough to cover this use case? To realize such integrations, we need more than APIs.

1.2 Integration with APIs and Events

Today, APIs are widely used, even for use cases that go beyond merely reading and writing data on a server application. APIs are not enough for the evolving expectations of API consumers. The apps of API consumers need to be responsive, event-based and react to changes in near real-time. When looking at the previous example, we see the following integration cases:

- Notify the client when a recurring payment fails

- Notify the client when an SMS text message could not be delivered

There are thousands of apps and simple integrations using APIs. To study them, just check out the so-called *recipes* on integration platforms such as IFTTT or Zapier. One more example:

- Notify the team via instant messaging when a new customer signs up

The pattern for these integrations is: an event triggers the integration workflow (e.g. customer signs up) and the integration uses the event data to call one or multiple APIs (e.g. instant messaging API). In this simple use case, we can clearly see the two essential concepts, which are required for integration: APIs and events.

- APIs allow for reading and writing data, calling functionality and starting processes. APIs connect us with actuators in the digital world that enable us to do and change things.

- Events allow for reacting to things happening in the environment. Events connect us with sensors in the digital world that wake us up, tell us that things have changed and what exactly has changed.

In a human analogy: APIs are the hands, events are the eyes. Life is much easier when we have both. Hands without eyes allow for blind action only - and eyes without hands allow us to see what needs to be done and when it needs to be done - without being able to carry out the necessary change. The same is true for APIs and events: APIs without events let us manipulate data, but not react to changes. Events without APIs let us pile up log data and even run analytics on it but without the capacity to act on the changes. If we want our APIs to be used, we need to provide both APIs and events - both hands and eyes to our consumers.

1.2.1 Case Study

Let's study the need for integration on the real-world case of TweetBuffer (www.tweetbuffer.com), a SaaS application for social media automation. Customers can start using the service for free and later upgrade to a premium version by paying a recurring monthly subscription fee. TweetBuffer uses a payment API to collect the monthly subscription fee. This API is provided by a third-party payment company. When the customer decides to purchase the premium version, TweetBuffer calls the API of the payment provider for initiating a recurring payment. In the API request, it passes the credit card data of the customer. In the response to this API call, TweetBuffer synchronously receives a payment confirmation for the first subscription fee. The payment provider takes care of charging the credit card of the customer on a monthly basis. Everything is nicely automated!

The interesting question in this scenario is: how does Tweet-Buffer know in subsequent months, whether the monthly subscription fee has been collected? The payment may have been declined for a number of reasons: the card may have been revoked in the meantime, or the credit limit may have been exceeded. TweetBuffer needs to react by informing the customer or even by locking her account.

For this reason, TweetBuffer needs events, which are sent by the payment provider. TweetBuffer needs to receive an event when the monthly charge for the recurring payment of any of the customers has failed. And if the payment provider were able to offer events in this manner, the payment API would become much more valuable and attractive to TweetBuffer as a result. TweetBuffer might even choose to switch to a payment provider that can offer events.

1.2.2 Advantages

After having established that it is essential to provide both APIs and events (see section 1.2), we can now talk about what it takes to gain a competitive advantage in the field of APIs and events.

Continuing in our analogy, we can say that hands and eyes are necessary to play the game. To win the game, however, hands and eyes need to be well-coordinated. Providing events which are well-coordinated with the available APIs is a competitive advantage for API providers and allows them to differentiate. What does coordination between APIs and events mean?

- For each method, endpoint, and action an API provider exposes, it should strive to provide a matching event. In general, one can say, the better the event coverage, the more opportunities for integration exist, and the more attractive the API becomes as a product.

- Another aspect of the coordination is that the APIs for managing webhooks need to blend in naturally with the overall API portfolio. The APIs for managing webhooks should follow REST constraints as far as possible, and they should be protected with the same security mechanisms as other APIs in the portfolio.

Moreover, API providers can gain a competitive advantage by supporting non-functional properties. And I am not only talking about reliability, availability, performance or security here, as those are essential and must be taken care of by all API providers. A competitive advantage can be gained with an amazing developer experience.

As it seems, the importance of an excellent developer experience is often forgotten or not taken seriously. So if you agree that developer experience is a differentiating factor for both APIs and events, then it is relatively easy to get a foot up on the competition.

A great design of the API portfolio, the events and event infrastructure is the most important factor for ensuring a great developer experience. It makes events easy and intuitive to use. And if using events is intuitive, API consumers don't want to read and don't need to read the documentation on the API portal. That is not to say that the documentation on the API portal is not important, it certainly is very important, but we should strive for API consumers not spending a lot of their precious time, reading reference documentation on our API portal. Instead, we should strive for API consumers building apps and integrations with our APIs and events.

Events are notoriously hard to test and debug. So anything we can do to improve testing and debugging of events will improve the developer experience a lot and will help our API to stand out in the minds of developers. A few examples for improving debugging and testing are:

- Providing test data or a sandbox environment

- Providing the ability to inspect event requests and responses on the API portal

- Providing the ability to trigger test events from the API portal or via API call

To gain a deeper understanding of the challenges involved in testing and debugging webhooks, have a look at chapter 7.

1.2.3 Challenges

Today, we have a good understanding of how APIs work and how they should be designed. But designing events and an event delivery infrastructure that complement the APIs is still quite challenging.

What makes event delivery so difficult and challenging? The difficulty is the *inversion of control*. Typically the client is in control and calls APIs. But in order to be notified by events, the client has to sit there and wait for events from the server. It is the Hollywood principle at work: *"Don't call us, we'll call you."* So in fact, for event delivery, the client becomes the server, and the server becomes the client. The client now needs to fulfill all the constraints that we would typically impose on a server. This includes all the non-functional properties such as reliability, availability, performance, and security. And then there is the challenge that the client (which now has to become a server) is developed by the consumer, not by the API provider.

There are a number of approaches that help us solve this technical challenge, as we will see in chapter 2. And one of the approaches is the webhooks approach which we will study in detail in this book (see sections 1.3 and chapter 3).

1.3 Webhooks in a Nutshell

Webhooks solve the event delivery challenge (see section 1.2.3) by letting the client register an HTTP endpoint that will be called by the API provider anytime an event happens. To explain webhooks, let's compare them to widely known concepts, such as *callback functions* and *event handlers*.

Webhooks can be compared to *event handlers*. Event handlers are typically used in frameworks for graphical user interfaces or interactive websites. An example of such an event handler: *when the user presses the return key, the main menu should open.* And if the user does not press the return button? Well, then nothing should happen at all, so there is a lot of waiting going on. The beauty of an event handler is that it does not need to concern itself with the waiting part. It is supported by an *event handler infrastructure* which calls the event handler when the event has occurred, and the event data is passed along with the call. A webhook can be seen as a special type of event handler because it works across application boundaries. The webhook neither needs to run on a particular operating system, nor on the same server, nor in the same browser. The webhook may be deployed on a remote computer, in a remote location, or in the cloud – as long as the webhook can be reached via HTTP and the web.

Webhooks can also be compared to *callback functions*. Callback functions receive events, process them and trigger further actions based on the event. Whoever wants to receive an event, writes a callback function and registers the callback function in the application generating the event. Callback functions are called, whenever something interesting happens in the application. Webhooks are very similar to callback functions, but instead of being a local function on the same machine, they are HTTP endpoints on a remote machine.

Based on what we have learned from the comparisons above, there are distinct responsibilities with webhooks. Clients (1) implement the webhook, i.e., define the actions that need to happen when the event occurs and (2) subscribe (i.e., register) the webhook for the desired event. API providers (1) define the possible events, (2) manage the subscriptions of webhooks to events and (3) deliver the events to the subscribed webhooks as they occur.

1.4 Contents of this Book

As we have seen, the needs for integration are evolving: integration needs to be responsive, event-based and react to changes in near real-time. By providing APIs alone, these needs cannot be fulfilled anymore. Any API provider who wants to offer integration capabilities, needs to offer both APIs and events. But how do we realize events in an API context? In this book, we explore this question and provide some best practices and actionable advice on providing both APIs and events that developers love to use.

In chapter 2, we study several approaches for realizing events, such as Polling, Long Polling, Webhooks, HTTP Streaming, Server-Sent Events, WebSockets, WebSub and GraphQL Subscriptions. All of these approaches have their advantages and disadvantages.

But when it comes to realizing events for RESTful APIs, the most common approach we observe in the field are webhooks. This is why we focus on webhooks in this book. In chapter 3, we study the webhooks concepts and the overall architecture of a webhooks infrastructure. In chapter 4, we study the non-functional requirements of a webhooks infrastructure, in areas such as security, reliability and developer experience.

How do well-known API providers design webhooks? In chapter 6, we examine the webhook infrastructure provided by GitHub, BitBucket, Stripe, Slack, and Intercom.

Based on the non-functional requirements, best practices, and the webhooks we observed from well-known API providers, we propose a concrete webhook design in chapter 5. But simply offering webhooks next to an API portfolio is not sufficient. APIs and the webhooks infrastructure need to be well-coordinated. We show how to integrate webhooks into a RESTful API portfolio and express our design using the OpenAPI[1][5] description language.

Finally, there is one more practical piece of advice. In chapter 7, we provide some practical tips and tools for developing, debugging, and testing webhooks.

---

[1]used to be called *Swagger*

2 Alternative Approaches to Realize Events

This book focuses on webhooks as the primary solution for realizing events since it is the most widely used approach. There are, however, alternative approaches which might be worth studying in the context of your specific use case. But if you only want to learn about webhooks, without looking left and right, feel free to jump ahead to chapter 3.

The basic patterns for realizing events are the *interrupt pattern* and the *polling pattern*. In approaches with the interrupt pattern (see sections 2.3, 2.4, 2.5, 2.6, and 2.7), the client is notified by an external event source when something interesting happens. The external event source is responsible for event execution. In approaches with the polling pattern (see sections 2.1 and 2.2), the client needs to figure out when something interesting happens, so the complete responsibility for event execution is with the client.

2.1 Short Polling

In the short polling approach, the client asks at regular intervals for a new status from the server. It works roughly as follows. The client asks the server: "Got news?" ... "Got any news now?" ... "How about now?" The server needs to provide an API that serves status information. If the server has a new status available, it sends the new status as a response to the API call. If the server has no new data available, it just sends an

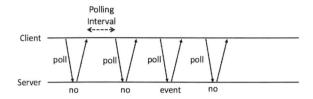

Figure 2.1: Timeline for Short Polling

empty response. This standard polling approach is sometimes also called *short polling* (to distinguish it from *long polling*, described in section 2.2).

An important design parameter is the *polling interval*. Setting an appropriate polling interval is critically important for this approach. Short polling intervals have the advantage of a near-real-time synchronization. The disadvantage of short polling intervals is the relatively high load imposed on the systems (client, server) and the network. Lots of data that has been unchanged and was read before will be transferred again. It does not scale for large numbers of clients.

HTTP caching might interfere with polling. Thus the HTTP header `Cache-Control` should be set to the value `no-cache`.

2.1.1 Advantages

The polling approach is a good choice for synchronization if the data consistency of the client depends on the reliability of event delivery, and if it is important that no updates are missed by the client.

Also, polling is quite universally applicable, since it does not put any constraints on the system. On some systems, it is not possible to receive notifications that are initiated by an external system because of firewalls that do not allow exposing any endpoints. In this case, the client needs to poll. So polling is

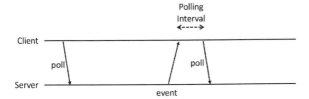

Figure 2.2: Timeline for Long Polling

sometimes the only viable option for realizing events.

2.1.2 Disadvantages

With a polling approach, the server typically needs to keep several connections simultaneously, which usually would require lots of resources. The server needs to be configured to limit resource usage and, e.g., not use a dedicated thread for each open connection and not create a new HTTP connection for each connection.

Even though threads can be shared and HTTP connections can be reused, some latency is introduced, and resources are used wastefully.

This approach does not provide an event data structure. Such a data structure is necessary and needs to be provided by the provider of the events.

2.2 Long Polling

Long polling is a variant of the polling pattern that attempts to fix some of the disadvantages of short polling, especially the fact that clients get an empty response when no data is available.

With long polling, the client sends an initial polling request, but the established HTTP communication channel is kept open, and the server does not send any response back as long as there is no data available. The server waits to send the response until an event occurs. From the client's perspective, the API call blocks. From the server's perspective, the connection is idle, i.e., there is no traffic going over the wire. This situation can only be changed by one of two incidents:

(1) An event occurs, and the response is sent back. The client needs to send another request, to be ready for receiving the next event.

(2) There is no event, and a timeout occurs. Unfortunately, HTTP calls cannot be blocked for an arbitrary period. The network stack limits blocking time and declares the communication dead after a *timeout period*, which is the maximum idle waiting time. The client also needs to send a request, to be ready for receiving the next event.

In either case, the client needs to send a new request. It may choose to send the request immediately or wait for the time specified in the polling interval before sending the next request.

One might think that very high timeout values would be a solution, but in practice, they are often not possible. Since the connection might be idle for a longer period of time, it might get dropped by a proxy or firewall. To prevent this, we activate the *TCP Keep-Alive* option for long polling.

There is also an optimization opportunity. If multiple events are waiting on the server to be delivered to the client, they should be delivered in batch to minimize message latency.

2.2.1 Advantages

The client can be alerted almost instantly with low latency, due to two reasons: (1) The client does not need to wait for the polling interval of normal polling. (2) Since the connection has already been established, the client does not need to wait for the HTTP connection to be established.

Long polling shares many advantages with the short polling approach (see section 2.1.1), such as reliability, data consistency and being feasible in many situations.

2.2.2 Disadvantages

The long polling approach uses resources a bit more economically than short polling, but by and large, the same disadvantages can be observed as in the short polling approach (see section 2.1.2).

2.3 HTTP Streaming

HTTP Streaming keeps the HTTP connection open for an indefinite period. The client initiates the connection, and the server waits until data is available. When data is available, the server sends event data. In contrast to long polling, the server does not close the connection after the event data has been sent. It keeps the connection alive, thus allowing the next event to be sent across the same connection. Ideally, the connection is never closed. However, errors might occur, so the client needs to have a mechanism to reinitiate the connection, similar to polling.

In HTTP 1.0 the streaming mode is the default mode since the client reads until the server closes the connection. The server just sends a response without the `Content-Length` HTTP Header.

In HTTP 1.1 there are two options to realize streaming. The first option is to set the `Connection` HTTP Header to `close`. This mode tells the client to read until the connection is explicitly closed. Another option to realize streaming in HTTP 1.1 is by setting the `Transfer-Encoding` HTTP Header of the response to the value `chunked`. Once the response has been opened with this header, each event can be sent as a chunk over the same connection. An HTTP chunk consists of the length of the event data, a `CR/LF`, and the actual event data. To close the stream, the server sends a final chunk of size 0.

2.3.1 Advantages

Streaming has a very low overhead regarding size: Only the chunk size needs to be added for each event. The worst case latency is as long as that of long polling, assuming that network intermediaries do not aggregate the chunks.

2.3.2 Disadvantages

Network intermediaries such as proxies or gateways might aggregate the chunks and only forward them, after all chunks have been received on their end. In this case, HTTP streaming will not work for delivering events.

This approach does not provide an event data structure. Such a data structure is necessary and needs to be provided by the provider of the events.

2.4 Server-Sent Events

With Server-Sent Events (SSE) the server sends events as an event stream and clients can subscribe to this event stream[2]. Technically, this approach is built on top of the HTTP streaming mechanism (see section 2.3). SSE supports mono-directional (server to client) communication and comes with error handling capabilities. It uses the content-type `text/event-stream` .

The events are encoded as text. Consecutive events are separated by two newlines (`\n\n`). Events consist of attributes, and each attribute of an event is separated by a newline (`\n`) from the next attribute. The attributes are key-value pairs, separated by a colon (`:`). Supported attribute keys are `event`, `data`, `id`, and `retry`.

Here is an example of a minimal event, consisting of merely one data attribute:

```
data: hello world\n\n
```

Here is an example of an event, consisting of several data attributes:

```
data: first attribute\n
data: second attribute\n\n
```

Here is an example of an event, consisting of an id, an event type, and two data attributes:

```
id: 12345
event: newuser
data: {user name : JohnDoe}\n
data: {user name : JohnDoe2}\n\n
```

2.4.1 Advantages

SSE has a low latency. SSE is also relatively well supported by modern browsers (although with limitations: the headers cannot be overwritten) and it can be consumed by client-side JavaScript. SSE can be used via the `EventSource` object in modern browsers.

2.4.2 Disadvantages

The server does not notice when a client gets disconnected. To mitigate this disadvantage, a heartbeat mechanism needs to be set up manually.

2.5 WebSockets

WebSockets is a TCP-based protocol providing a full duplex communication link between client and server[1]. WebSockets are available as an unprotected variant (`ws://`) and as a secure, TLS-protected variant (`wss://`).

Figure 2.3: WebSub Concepts

2.5.1 Advantages

WebSockets are relatively well supported by most modern browsers, and it can also be consumed by client-side JavaScript via the WebSocket object in modern browsers.

2.5.2 Disadvantages

WebSockets are not based on HTTP (only TCP), and thus some proxies or gateways won't allow it without manual configuration. There is no explicit support for events in WebSockets. However, events can just be implemented as JSON text, which is sent via WebSockets. WebSockets does not provide any standards for error handling.

2.6 WebSub

WebSub[1] [6] uses callbacks to distribute events from so-called publishers to subscribers. It introduces the concept of a hub, which is an intermediary between publisher and subscriber (see Figure 2.3). Publishers deliver their events to the hub. The hub manages the subscriptions and validates them. The hub also forwards the events to the subscribers. Publisher and subscriber do not interact directly, but only via the hub.

When a subscriber wants to receive events from a publisher, it cannot subscribe directly with the publisher; it needs to subscribe via the hub, which is responsible for the publisher and handles its subscriptions.

---

[1]WebSub was formerly known as PubSubHubbub.

Discovery How does a subscriber find the correct hub? It uses a process called discovery. To support discovery, the publisher provides the link to its hub in the `<Link>` tags in its HTML headers or the `Link` HTTP header, annotated with `rel=hub` according to [8]. In the same manner, the event type is encoded in the `<Link>` tags or `Link` HTTP header, annotated with `rel=self`. The subscriber performs discovery by parsing the messages and extracting the link to the hub and the topic name.

Subscription The subscriber subscribes to the event on the hub, by sending a data structure to the hub, which includes the topic, the callback URL, the mode (possible values are: `subscribe` or `unsubscribe`) and a shared secret, which the client can choose. The hub (1) validates, (2) confirms and (3) reconfirms the subscription.

- For the validation step (1), the hub performs some optional checks on the submitted data and confirms the subscription request with a `202 Accepted` HTTP status code.

- The confirmation step (2) is performed to verify the subscription intent of the subscriber. To verify the intent, the hub sends a confirmation data structure to the callback URL, which includes the requested topic name, the requested mode (`subscribe` or `unsubscribe`) and a challenge. The challenge is a parameter with a random value that is generated by the server. The callback service may check the subscription information and needs to return the challenge value with a `2xx` HTTP status code.

- The optional reconfirmation step (3) is performed at regular intervals, to ensure the subscription is still required. On a technical level, the reconfirmation works exactly as the confirmation.

31

Event Delivery   When a new event is published, the publisher sends it to the hub, and the hub distributes it to the subscribers with the POST HTTP method. The body is expected to be the complete resource that corresponds to the event type. But before the hub forwards the event to the subscribers, it signs it using the shared secret of the respective subscriber. It transmits the signature in the `X-Hub-Signature` HTTP Header. On receipt, the subscriber recomputes the signature and compares the computed value against the header value and only accepts it if the signatures match. The hub expects the subscriber to return a 2xx HTTP status code to confirm delivery of the event.

2.6.1 Advantages

A lot of best practices are incorporated in WebSub. It can thus be considered to be a good example and an inspiration for implementing your webhooks.

WebSub introduces the concept of the hub, which introduces a level of indirection in the event flow, thus allowing for migration of the data without affecting the subscription.

2.6.2 Disadvantages

The hub endpoint incorporates a couple of HTTP concepts, but it cannot be considered RESTful. For example, subscription resource cannot be created or deleted with the appropriate methods.

The WebSub standard targets generic web content, it is not explicitly developed for events in an API context.

2.7 GraphQL Subscriptions

GraphQL is a *query language* for APIs. The language allows us to structure the interaction between frontend on the client and a backend on the server. The language provides primitives for specifying the data served by the API, retrieving data, writing data and getting notified when data changes. And of course, it is the later feature, getting notified by GraphQL subscriptions, that we use to realize events.

The client sends a subscription request to the GraphQL API. The client specifies in the request both the event type (`bookAdded` in the example) to be observed and the data (`id` and `title`), which should be sent from the server to the client, when the event is triggered.

```
subscription {
  bookAdded {
    id
    title
  }
}
```

In the above example, a client requests a subscription called `bookAdded` from the GraphQL API. The client uses this subscription to be notified whenever new books are available on the server. The client even specifies, which fields of the newly added book are relevant to be included in the notification: `id` and `title`.

What triggers a notification? In most cases, a notification is triggered by a modification of the data that is served by the API. This means that an event handler (for `bookAdded` in our example) needs to be installed inside the implementation of the API that modifies the data. It sends the event to the client. In rare cases, a notification could be triggered by an external event, which is not directly accessible inside the graph or only accessible in aggregated form.

2.7.1 Advantages

The GraphQL framework provides a lot of boilerplate code for event subscription. So it is fast and reliable to implement events with GraphQL.

The client can influence, which fields should be delivered and which fields are not required. So the client can determine in the typical GraphQL manner, which fields it needs.

2.7.2 Disadvantages

The subscriptions in GraphQL only make sense, when the API is already realized with GraphQL. When extending a REST API with events, it does not make sense, to combine the existing API with GraphQL subscriptions.

3 Using Webhooks to Realize Events

After having surveyed a number of approaches for realizing events in chapter 2, we now focus on webhooks as the preferred concept for realizing events. Webhooks are the most widely used approach for solving the event delivery challenge (see section 1.2.3) and realizing events in combination with REST APIs.

So what are webhooks? Webhooks are neither a technology that you can buy and install nor a standard that is written down by a committee. What we call webhooks is merely a collection of concepts and a collection of best practices based on these concepts. In this chapter, we build a foundation by defining these concepts and showing how they are related and in the following chapters, we share the best practices for webhooks.

We need to make a distinction between the terms *webhooks* and *webhook endpoint*. Webhooks refers to the overall concept of sending events to webhook endpoints. Webhook endpoints are the services, which are implemented on the client-side to process the events.

3.1 Webhooks Roles

Webhooks are typically used in combination with an API. In the context of APIs, there are clearly defined roles (see Figure 3.1): the role of the *API provider* and the role of the *API client*. The client can initiate API calls, and also needs to get notified when something happens on the side of the API provider.

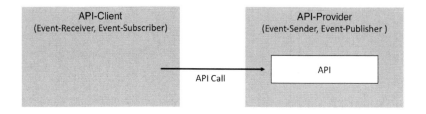

Figure 3.1: API Concepts

3.1.1 API Provider

The API provider becomes an *event publisher* by offering events. The API provider does this, by offering a *subscription API*, so clients can subscribe to the events it publishes.

It needs to provide at least an *event sender endpoint* to send out or publish events. This turns the API provider into an *event sender*. The API provider may also offer an *event history API*, to offer a possibility to recover missed events.

3.1.2 API Client

The API client becomes an *event subscriber*, by subscribing to an event, i.e., voicing its intent to get notified when an event occurs. After subscribing, the client just needs to wait for an event to arrive. When an event arrives, the API client becomes an *event receiver* by processing the incoming event. In order to become an event subscriber and event receiver, the API client needs to offer an *event receiver endpoint* which is another name for *webhook endpoint*.

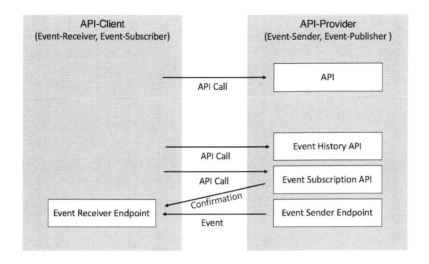

Figure 3.2: Webhook Concepts

3.2 Webhooks Concepts

An overview of the webhooks concepts is visualized in figure 3.2. When reading about the concepts in the following sections, refer back to this figure.

3.2.1 Events

Events occur in the application on the side of the API provider and indicate that something has happened or changed. An event may occur internally in the application, externally or may be caused by an API call. In either case, the API provider uses its *event sender endpoint* to send the event to all registered *event receiver endpoints* of the respective API clients.

The event is described by a message, which contains meta-data about the event such as its *event type*. The event type classifies the event and the change that occurred. The message may even contain the actual data of the resource that is affected by the change. When clients subscribe, they specify – among other things – the event type. In the context of an event subscription, the event type is also called *topic*.

3.2.2 Event Sender Endpoint

When an event of a certain event type occurs on the side of the API provider, the *event sender endpoint* sends out the event. It sends the event to the event receiver endpoints (see section 3.2.3) that are subscribed to the given type of event (see section 3.2.1).

3.2.3 Event Receiver Endpoint

The *event receiver endpoint* is sometimes also called *webhook endpoint*. The mechanism of the event receiver endpoint is similar to a callback function in programming: pass a reference to a function, and this function gets called when the event occurs. Now, for a webhook, this callback function is realized in the form of an API, which is implemented on the client-side. Its task is to process the incoming events.

When an event occurs on the side of the API provider, the event sender endpoint sends out the event to all the *event receiver endpoints* that have subscribed to this type of event.

What is so special about the event receiver endpoint? The signature of the endpoint is specified by the API provider, but it needs to be implemented on the client-side according to the specifications of the API provider: the endpoint needs to be able to interpret the event messages sent by the API provider, and it needs to respond to the API provider. Both the expected responses and the event messages are specified by the API provider. Not only does the event receiver endpoint have to conform to the functional specification of the API provider, but it also has to fulfill a number of non-functional properties, a precondition for secure, reliable, highly available and developer-friendly APIs.

3.2.4 Event Subscription API

A client can indicate its interest in receiving events of a certain event type, by registering or subscribing to the event type. To subscribe, the client creates a new subscription resource via the *subscription API*. Among other attributes, the *subscription resource* contains the URL of the *event receiver endpoint* (see section 3.2.3) and the *event type* (see section 3.2.1).

Event subscription is offered via the subscription API described here and via a webhook dashboard described in section 3.2.6.

3.2.5 Event History API

A client may miss some of the events that are addressed to it, e.g. because its event receiver endpoint (see section 3.2.3) is temporarily unavailable or overloaded. These events are stored in the event history database on the side of the API provider.

With the *event history API*, the client can access the event history database and obtain a list of recent events that were addressed to it. The client can manually reconcile the missed events based on the data delivered by the event history API. The event history API typically offers the possibility to filter the returned events, e.g., by event type, by delivery status or by timestamp.

3.2.6 Webhook Dashboard

The webhook dashboard is a part of the API portal. Access to the webhook dashboard is restricted to registered API consumers.

The webhook dashboard is a user interface for managing webhook subscriptions, viewing webhook logs, and viewing the event history. On this dashboard, new subscriptions can be created, and existing subscriptions can be inspected, tested and adapted. To support testing, the webhooks dashboard offers API consumers to send synthetic events to test their clients and receiver endpoints.

3.3 Webhooks Interactions

In the previous section, we have introduced the concepts that are used in a webhooks infrastructure. In this section, we study the relationships and interactions between these concepts. The main interactions are event delivery (see section 3.3.1) and event subscription (see section 3.3.2).

3.3.1 Event Delivery

This interaction delivers events from the API provider to the API client. It involves the event receiver (see section 3.2.3) on the client side (see section 3.1.2). And on the side of the API provider (see section 3.1.1), it involves the event sender (see section 3.2.2), the event history database (see section 3.2.5) and the server application.

The interactions for the delivery of events are visualized in figure 3.3 in the form of an interaction diagram. The interactions are numbered:

(1) On the side of the API provider, the server app performs a task which generates an internal event. The server app forwards the internal event to the event sender.

(2) The event sender checks for each internal event, which API clients have subscribed to this type of event and to which event receiver URL the event needs to be sent. The event sender

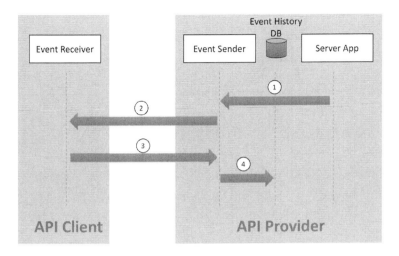

Figure 3.3: Interactions for Event Delivery

obtains this information from the subscription database. If multiple subscribers are registered for the same event type, multiple events need to be sent out, one for each subscriber. The event sender transforms the event from the internal structure into the externally communicated event structure, including all metadata and client specific signature. Then the event sender sends the individually signed event to the respective URL of the event receiver. The sender needs to make sure that failure to deliver to one of the receivers does not affect the delivery of the other events.

(3) When the event receiver gets the event, it validates the event, schedules it for processing and confirms the receipt of the event within a certain timeframe.

(4) The event sender records the event including its delivery status in the event history database.

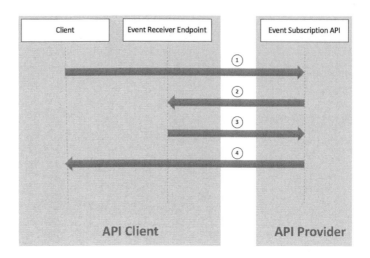

Figure 3.4: Interactions for Event Subscription

3.3.2 Event Subscription

With this interaction, the client indicates its interest in receiving events. Involved in this interaction are the client (see section 3.1.2), the event receiver endpoint (see section 3.2.3) and the event subscription API (see section 3.2.4).

The client registers an appropriate event receiver endpoint using the subscription API. The necessary interactions between the subscription API and the receiver endpoint are visualized in figure 3.4. The interactions are numbered:

Every time the subscription is changed via the API (1), the subscription change needs to be confirmed by the client (2), and the change is only executed if the client confirms the change (3). Then the response of the subscription API is sent back to the client (4).

Some things need to have happened before event subscription. Before event subscription, the consumer needs to have developed an event receiver endpoint that can process events according to the specifications of the API provider. It needs to have made this endpoint publicly available, and operate it.

3.4 Coordination of APIs and Webhooks

As we have alluded to before, it is important that APIs and webhooks do not just co-exist next to each other, but that they are coordinated. What does coordination between APIs and webhooks mean? It means recognizing that there is a relation between the actions that can be performed via API and the state transitions that can be observed via events (see section 3.4.1). To provide optimal possibilities for integration, we propose that an API provider should strive to provide matching events for each API (see section 3.4.2).

3.4.1 Relation between APIs and Events

A server application changes its state due to interactions with the users or interactions with the environment. A server application may allow clients to read or change its application state via API calls. A server application may also allow clients to observe changes in its application state and react to state changes via events. So there is a relation between the actions of the API and the events that can be observed.

3.4.2 Coordinating APIs and Events

We propose that an API provider should strive to provide a matching event for each state transition, i.e., for each method, endpoint, and action it exposes via API. In general, one can say, the better the event coverage, the more opportunities for integration exist and the more attractive the API becomes as a product.

4 Non-Functional Requirements of Webhooks

Fulfilling the non-functional requirements for webhooks should not be an afterthought but should guide the design decisions from the start. All webhooks need to be reliable, secure, available and developer-friendly. These non-functional requirements, however, may be weighted differently depending on (1) the type of application offering the webhooks infrastructure and (2) the event data exposed via the webhooks. To see in real-world examples how different types of application value different non-functional properties, and how this reflects on their webhooks design, check out chapter 6.

The channel between event sender and event receiver is unreliable, and events may get lost or duplicated. In section 4.1, we study methods to make webhooks more reliable.

Events provide insights into the data of end users, API consumers, and API provider. This data and the computing infrastructure need to be protected. In section 4.2, we study how to secure webhooks.

Webhooks may create heavy workloads for connected clients and the webhooks infrastructure. Nevertheless, they need to be available and have good performance characteristics. We show how to achieve this in section 4.3.

4.1 Reliability

The channel between event sender and event receiver is unreliable: event data might not arrive at all (e.g. due to network issues, due to problems on the sender-side, or due to problems on the receiver-side) or might be duplicated (e.g. due to retry logic). In this section, we study some strategies to improve the reliability of event delivery (see section 4.1.1). We also propose some mechanisms to support those reliability strategies on the side of the sender (see sections 4.1.2, 4.1.3, 4.1.4) and receiver (see section 4.1.5).

4.1.1 Reliability Strategies

If the event sender calls the receiver in a fire-and-forget mode and an error occurs in sender or receiver, the event data will be lost. There are several mitigation strategies for improving the reliability of webhooks with reasonable effort. These strategies should be combined.

4.1.1.1 Event Receiver Specification

Information and expectations are the first line of defense. The API provider needs to specify the event receiver interface (e.g. with an OpenAPI specification of the receiver endpoint) and its behavior (e.g. with a detailed documentation on the API portal). Especially the API provider needs to document, what the event sender considers to be a failure case during event delivery.

4.1.1.2 Thin Events and Pulling

A strategy to improve the reliability of event delivery is to combine thin events (see section 5.2.1.1) with pulling data. The receiver does not rely on the data in the event. It uses the event merely as a notification, indicating that something of interest has changed on the server. The client pulls the changed data directly via API call from the server.

4.1.1.3 Retry Mechanism

A retry mechanism actively attempts to deliver previously failed events. As soon as a retry mechanism comes into play, it cannot be guaranteed that the message is delivered only once, the message may be delivered several times. Thus, if a retry mechanism is used, the receiver is required to be idempotent (see section 3.2.3).

4.1.1.4 Event History and Reconciliation

Another strategy is to deliver events in a best-effort attempt, record any delivery attempts and reconcile any missed events. The sender needs to provide the data for reconciliation. This approach allows for the use of thin or thick events. Events are delivered with best effort. The sender records all events that were sent out in an event history database and indicates whether or not they have been delivered successfully to the receiver. So when the server reports an error or timeout, the event in the event history is stored together with a flag indicating that it has not yet been delivered. Via the event history API, this data can be made available to the respective receiver for manual event reconciliation. It is the responsibility of the receiver to periodically check the event history for undelivered events.

4.1.2 Sender: Recognizing Delivery Errors

The event sender has to deal with various implementations of receivers, and they are likely to have different behavior. It is important that the sender documents, what it considers to be a failure case in the receiver, including timeout values and error codes. A good place for this documentation is the API portal, where ideally an OpenAPI specification of the receiver endpoint is hosted. Typical delivery errors that can be observed on the event sender:

- Timeouts: the receiver endpoint does not send any response back. There are several reasons for this. The request may have gotten lost, the receiver may have run into a problem while processing the event (e.g. processing may just take very long) or the response may have gotten lost.

- Error response: the receiver endpoint responds with anything but a 2xx HTTP status code, e.g. a 3xx, 4xx or 5xx.

The event sender needs to react to the event delivery errors listed above:

- When a timeout occurs or when a 5xx status code is returned, the event is flagged as not-delivered (see section 4.1.3) and may get scheduled for retry (see section 4.1.4).

- When a 4xx or a 3xx status code is returned, the event is flagged as not-delivered (see section 4.1.3). Human intervention is likely needed to analyze the situation: Is the receiver endpoint no longer available? Has the receiver endpoint moved? Is the event still required by the receiver? If this class of error has occurred several times within a given timeframe, an automated email can be sent once per timeframe to the registered developer. HTTP redirects indicated by a 3xx status code should not be followed since this is a minor security risk.

4.1.3 Sender: Keeping an Event History

The sender records all events that were sent out in an event history database. For each event, the sender records the timestamp of the first delivery attempt, the timestamp of the most recent delivery attempt, the number of delivery attempts so far and the delivery status.

Via the event history API (see section 5.7) the records of the event history database can be made available to the respective receiver for manual event reconciliation. The event history API delivers each event that has occurred in the recent past and has been attempted to be sent to the respective receiver. By filtering the events according to their delivery status, the event history API enables clients to manually reconcile missed events, e.g. after an application failure.

4.1.4 Sender: Retry Mechanism

A retry mechanism is an optional feature of an event sender. It starts another attempt to deliver an event that previously could not be delivered. For the retry mechanism to work, we need a clear understanding of what the sender interprets as success and failure from the receiver (see section 4.1.4.1), the receiver needs to be idempotent (see section 4.1.4.2), and the event history database needs to be kept up to date (see section 4.1.4.3). Typical design parameters of a retry mechanism are the retry interval (see section 4.1.4.4), the maximum number of retries (see section 4.1.4.5) and the final action (see section 4.1.4.6) to be performed if the event could not be delivered.

4.1.4.1 Failure Classification

For a retry mechanism to work, we need a clear understanding of what the sender interprets as success and failure from the receiver (see section 4.1.2). When the error is a timeout or a response with 5xx HTTP status code, a retry makes sense (see section 4.1.2). Retries should not be sent, when other HTTP status codes are returned, such as 3xx or 4xx.

4.1.4.2 Idempotent Receiver

Due to the retry mechanisms, the receiver may get the same event multiple times. To deal with this situation, the receiver endpoint needs to be idempotent (see section 5.4.1.1). It needs to recognize a duplicated event, produce the same output as the first time around and not cause any side effects.

4.1.4.3 Update Event History Database

The sender keeps one entry for each event in the event history database (see section 4.1.3). When the event delivery is retried, no new entry is added to the event history database, but the existing event is updated with the latest timestamp, the latest number of delivery attempts and the latest delivery state.

The retry should be based on the data of the event history. If the event has been processed in the meantime because the receiver has manually processed the event history data, the retry mechanism should be stopped.

4.1.4.4 Retry Interval

The retry interval is the time that passes between two consecutive retries. The retry interval should not be fixed, but adaptive and get longer with each unsuccessful retry. The exponential back-off algorithm can be used to calculate the retry interval, as it doubles the retry interval on each delivery attempt. We also add some jitter to the retry interval. The jitter avoids that all failed requests retry at the same time, which may result in a temporary overload.

4.1.4.5 Maximum Retries

Even if an exponential back-off algorithm is used, retrying cannot go on forever. At some point, we have to give up and declare the permanent failure of the delivery. So how many times should we retry or how long should we retry until we give up? The exact number of retries depends on the type of application. In the wild (see chapter 6), we have seen maximum retries in the range from 3 to 100.

4.1.4.6 Final Action

When the maximum retries have been consumed, and the last retry has also been unsuccessful, there should be a final action before forgetting the event. Typically, the final action involves sending an email notification to the registered developer on the client side.

Retrying is a good solution if we can assume that the delivery problems are temporary. If webhooks of clients, however, consistently and permanently fail, and there are no successfully delivered events, then we should at least temporarily disable the subscription or event delivery.

4.1.5 Receiver: Resynchronization of Events

If the receiver has missed some events, e.g. due to a downtime, it has two choices: (1) rely on the retry mechanism to resynchronize passively, as described in section 4.1.5.1 or (2) use the event history API to resynchronize actively, as described in section 4.1.5.2.

4.1.5.1 Passive Resynchronization

If the sender has a retry mechanism and the maximum retry period has not passed for the missed events, the receiver may just wait for the next retry by the sender. The advantage of this approach is that it requires no effort on the receiver side, the disadvantage is that it might take some time until all missed events have been processed, especially when an exponential back-off algorithm is implemented in the sender.

4.1.5.2 Active Resynchronization

In case of a longer problem in the receiver endpoint, the retry mechanisms may not be able to deliver the event and will eventually give up. The events that failed to deliver are not lost and are still available. The receiver may use the event history API to get the list of events that could not be delivered. The receiver processes these events in a batch process.

4.2 Security

There are several elements in the webhook infrastructure that require security considerations:

- How can the receiver ensure that the request originates from the correct sender?
    - The receiver endpoint needs to authenticate the sender.

- How can the receiver ensure that the request has not been manipulated?
    - The sender creates a signature based on the shared secret, the receiver recomputes the signature and compares the two signatures.

- How can the sender ensure that the event is delivered to the correct receiver?
    - The receiver needs to be authenticated, e.g., the receiver needs to support HTTPS and use a certificate that is signed by an official authority.

- How can the sender ensure that only the receiver can read the event?

– The transport channel should be encrypted, e.g. by
using HTTPS.

To create the appropriate level of security for event delivery,
we need to mitigate security-related risks both on the side of
the receiver (see section 4.2.1) and on the side of the sender
(see section 4.2.2). We also need to protect the APIs used in
the context of webhooks (see section 4.2.3) and especially the
subscription API (see section 4.2.4).

4.2.1 Receiver Endpoint Security

The API and webhook system is only as secure as the weak-
est link. The API provider can make sure that its systems are
reasonably secure, but it cannot enforce a level of security on
the API clients, i.e. event receivers, since event receivers are
designed and implemented by the clients. Thus one has to sus-
pect that the event receiver endpoints are a weak link in the
system. An event receiver endpoint has to fulfill the following
security-related requirements:

- Authenticate the sender of the events (see section 4.2.1.1)

- Ensure the authenticity of the event (see section 4.2.1.2)

- Ensure that the events cannot be read by unauthorized
  parties (see section 4.2.2.3)

- Make sure that the sender can authenticate the receiver
  (see section 4.2.1.4).

- Limit the access of the event receiver endpoint by IP whitelisting and keeping the receiver URL a secret (see section
  4.2.1.5).

4.2.1.1 Authentication of the Sender

Risk An attacker can impersonate the sender and send fake events to the receiver.

Mitigation When processing incoming events in the receiver, we need to make sure that the events originate from the correct sender, i.e., we need to authenticate the sender.

The receiver endpoint should support the best authentication mechanism, the sender can offer. If the sender offers to use a client certificate, then that should be used if the sender only offers HTTP Basic Authentication then that should be used.

The smallest common denominator is to authenticate the sender based on a username and password with HTTP Basic Authentication. In this setup, the receiver chooses username and password for the sender and shares it with the sender when subscribing. The sender applies this username and password pair when sending events.

4.2.1.2 Authenticity of the Event

Risk A faked event can be injected, or the data of an existing event can be manipulated.

Mitigation Making sure that the event data has not been tampered with is just the beginning. We usually want to ensure the authenticity of the event. To ensure the authenticity of the event, we ensure that the event has in fact been created by the sender (authentication), the sender cannot deny having sent the message (non-repudiation), and that the message has not been changed in transit (integrity).

This can be ensured by a cryptographic signature, a Hash-based Message Authentication Code (HMAC). The sender signs the event payload with the shared secret (i.e. computes the

HMAC value) and includes the resulting signature in an HTTP header (such as a `Signature` HTTP header or `X-Hub-Signature` HTTP header). The receiver validates the signature by recomputing the signature based on the received event payload and the shared secret. If the two signatures match, the computed signature and the received signature, we can assume that the message is authentic.

When computing and comparing signatures, it is a good idea to use secure cryptographic libraries, e.g. secure-compare to mitigate timing attacks.

4.2.1.3 Replay Attacks

Risk   The attacker may record traffic and play it back later.

Mitigation   Events need to contain a timestamp, and the event including the timestamp needs to be signed. Attackers cannot change this timestamp in the event without invalidating the signature.

So to detect replay attacks, receivers need to validate the signature and validate the timestamp attribute contained in the event. When validating the timestamp a tolerance of +/- 5 minutes should be applied.

4.2.1.4 Allowing the Sender to Authenticate the Receiver

Risk   An attacker may use a fake receiver to collect events.

Mitigation   To make it possible for the sender to verify the identity of the receiver, the receiver endpoint should be available via HTTPS with an SSL certificate. Sometimes self-signed certificates are used for receiver endpoints. Those, however, are not signed by a trusted authority and are thus not trustworthy.

It is essential to use an official SSL certificate from a trusted certificate authority.

4.2.1.5 Limit Traffic on Receiver Endpoint

Risk The event receiver endpoint might be the target of attacks against the client. Connection attempts from various sources strain the hardware and use up resources.

Mitigation: IP Whitelisting Clients should block incoming requests on their firewall and only allow requests from whitelisted IP addresses. Clients need to know the public IP address(es) of the event sender, so they can selectively open up their firewall for these IPs. The IPs of the event sender should be published on the API portal. Note, that this measure alone is insufficient, it should only be used together with other mechanisms. It is not a means to authenticate the sender, since IP addresses can be faked.

Mitigation: Endpoint URL as a Secret A very simple measure is to treat the endpoint URL as a secret. The client should choose a URL that is not guessable, e.g. by including some random elements. The URL should not be shared, advertised or be publicly documented.

4.2.2 Sender Endpoint Security

The sender needs to be sure, it communicates with the correct receiver.

4.2.2.1 Authentication of the Receiver

Risk A fake receiver endpoint receives the events.

Mitigation   The sender needs to validate the certificate of the receiver. Of course, the receiver needs to provide the certificate in the first place, as described in section 4.2.1.4.

4.2.2.2 Allowing the Receiver to Authenticate the Sender

Risk   An attacker can impersonate the sender and send fake events to the receiver.

Mitigation   The sender needs to prove its identity to the client, either via a client certificate or HTTP Basic Authentication.

4.2.2.3 Event Encryption

Risk   Sensitive business data may be exposed when transmitted unencrypted over insecure channels as part of a thick event. Unauthorized parties can eavesdrop on events and get access to the data they contain.

Mitigation   Mitigation strategies need to ensure that the sensitive data cannot be read by unauthorized parties. Encryption on the level of the transport channel (such as provided by HTTPS) or on message level would solve the issue.

Ideally, a secure and encrypted transport channel, such as HTTPS[9], is offered by the receiver and supported by the sender. If using HTTPS, it is always best to use an official certificate which is from a trusted certificate authority.

But from a practical perspective, implementing message encryption or providing an HTTPS-protected receiver endpoint is often not feasible for clients. When encryption is not available, we need to exclude the sensitive data from the event, or we can only allow thin events (see section 5.2.1.1). Clients can still access business data, but only by pulling it from protected APIs, which are accessible via a secure transport channel of the API provider.

4.2.3 General API Security

All APIs in the portfolio of the API provider should be protected with HTTPS [9] and OAuth [7] as described in [3]. This guideline also applies to the subscription API (see sections 4.2.4 and 5.5) and the event history API (see section 5.7).

4.2.4 Subscription API Security

Like any API on the server (see section 4.2.3), the subscription API needs to be protected by HTTPS [9] and OAuth [7].

In addition, there are some specific security risks in the subscription API that need to be taken care of. During subscription, we need to ensure that no one is using the callback feature of our sender as a tool for attacking our own or another system.

4.2.4.1 Authentication & Authorization

Risk   Just because a client is allowed to access the subscription API, does not allow him to subscribe to and receive arbitrary events. Sometimes a more fine-granular authorization on the level of event types is required, e.g. because some events contain more critical data than others.

Mitigation   The OAuth access token is used as an authentication of the client and as a coarse granular authorization to determine access to the subscription API. To realize fine granular authorization, OAuth scopes are used.

An event is typically associated with a resource. Access to this resource is only possible with a valid OAuth access token that has the right OAuth scope. Because of the association between resource and event and because they expose the same information, it makes a lot of sense to require the same OAuth scope for subscribing to the event, as is required for accessing the associated resource. The OAuth scopes are typically used as permissions and in this case, OAuth scopes are used as permissions for subscribing to a particular event. To see this security pattern in the wild, check out the subscription API of Slack described in section 6.2.

4.2.4.2 Attacks on Webhook Servers

Risk Someone can use webhooks to get into your server environments, by creating a subscription and using e.g. a local address as receiver endpoint. Since the event sender is part of our internal server network, the attacker can use webhooks to gain access to internal systems. Via the webhook dashboard, API providers often give the possibility to inspect the responses. In this case, the attacker can use the response data to gain insight into the internal server landscape to prepare further attacks.

Mitigation

1. Resolve the notification receivers addresses using DNS into a list of IPs. Then check each IP against a blacklist. This blacklist should contain the address of API portfolio, private network IP addresses (RFC 1918 addresses) and EC2 instance metadata.

2. Use a proxy for outgoing traffic, so it is not possible to get access to your server environment.

4.2.4.3 Attacks on Other Servers

Risk An attacker may abuse the event sender as a traffic generator to bombard an unsuspecting endpoint with traffic by subscribing this endpoint as a webhook. An attack can now be started by generating events. Events are sent to the target endpoint, and the target endpoint seems to be attacked by the event sender. In a first instance, the API provider is made responsible for the attack, since the traffic originates from its system.

Mitigation When the subscription API receives a subscription request, it needs to confirm the intent of the client to install the webhook. For this purpose, the subscription API sends a confirmation event to the webhook when it is in the process of registering a new webhook. It is very unlikely that an unsuspecting endpoint will process confirmation events properly. Thus an attacker's attempt to register an unsuspecting endpoint will fail.

Every webhook needs to be able to process confirmation events. A confirmation event is a regular event, of type `confirmation` (see section 5.2.1.5). In its payload, the event contains the subscription information (which has been received by the subscription API) and a random value, the so-called `challenge`.

The webhook has the opportunity to check the subscription information contained in the confirmation event. To confirm the subscription, the webhook needs to return the `challenge` value in the HTTP body with a **2xx** HTTP status code as a response.

If a webhook does not respond as expected to the confirmation request, i.e. sends the correct challenge value, the requested subscription operation (whether it is a PUT, POST or DELETE) is discarded.

4.3 Availability and Performance

4.3.1 Receiver: Prevent Event Flooding

Receiver endpoints might get flooded with events, especially when several topics have been assigned to the same receiver endpoint. It is the responsibility of the receiver to be prepared to handle large numbers of events and to be able to process the amounts of data that comes with these events.

The recommendation is to place incoming events into a queue and acknowledge the receipt of the event as quickly as possible, by sending a 202 `Accepted` status code to the sender. The events can be processed asynchronously out of the queue whenever there is free capacity. An exception to this pattern can be made if event processing has low complexity and executes fast. Under these circumstances, events could be processed immediately upon receipt.

For the receiver, this approach helps to smooth out the load of processing the events and puts the receiver back into the driver seat. The receiver can decide, how quickly it wants to process the events and how much resources it is willing to dedicate to it.

For the sender, it has the advantage that it frees up resources. When the sender acknowledges the receipt of the event, the connection can be closed, the event can be archived in the event history, the memory can be freed, and no further processing needs to be performed for this event.

Only the receiver can protect from event flooding, the sender cannot really influence that. But the sender can suffer from the negative consequences when the receiver does not handle this issue properly. So the sender needs to educate the receiver and make it as simple as possible for the receiver to handle this issue appropriately.

As a result of handling event flooding properly, the complete system has a higher likelihood of reaching a consistent state: (1) the sender knows that the event has reached the receiver (2) the likelihood of timeouts occurring is minimized (3) the need for performing retries is minimized.

4.3.2 Sender: Scaling

To deal with high load on the server side, the sender should be scalable. To achieve this, we split the sender into a controller and a number of stateless sender workers. The sender workers are responsible for sending an event request and reporting the response. The controller is responsible for assigning events to workers and for initiating the retry mechanism. With this separation of concerns, we can scale the number of workers as necessary.

4.3.3 Sender: Limit Number of Subscriptions

Each subscription uses up resources. Thus, the number of subscriptions per client is often limited, e.g. to a maximum of 250 subscriptions per client.

4.4 Developer Experience

The developer experience is an increasingly important aspect when designing APIs and the associated events. It seems that the importance of an excellent developer experience is often forgotten or not taken seriously. So if you agree that developer experience is a differentiating factor for both APIs and events, then it is relatively easy to get a foot up on the competition.

In section 4.4.1 we show what needs to be documented on the API portal, and in section 4.4.2 we talk about the specification of the client-side receiver endpoint that needs to be provided. In section 4.4.3 we show some ideas how on supporting developers, e.g. by providing test data, the ability to inspect event requests and the responses on your API portal, the ability to trigger test events via the API portal or via API call are just a few examples.

4.4.1 Documentation

All webhooks concepts and also the most important design decisions that were made for the webhooks of this specific provider, need to be documented on the API portal. The API portal should also contain the central definition of topics/event-types. The server-side APIs, i.e. the subscription API and the event history API need to be documented on the API portal, just as any other API in the API portfolio.

Security-related information needs to be documented very well. Consumers need to know the public IP address(es) of the event sender, e.g. to whitelist these IPs and open up their firewall. The IPs should be published on the API portal.

4.4.2 Receiver Specification

The specification of the client-side event receiver endpoint should be available as a machine-readable API description (such as OpenAPI[5], RAML, or Blueprint) and as a human-readable, HTML-rendered API reference documentation. Code generators or even SDKs should be made available, too. To see an example of a receiver specification in OpenAPI, check section 5.4.

4.4.3 Testing Support

Webhooks are notoriously difficult to test. Anything we can do to improve testing and debugging of webhooks will improve the developer experience a lot and will help our APIs and webhooks to stand out in the minds of developers.

4.4.3.1 Webhook Dashboard

The webhook dashboard (see section 3.2.6) is a part of the API portal, which allows subscription management via a web-based user interface. After logging in, clients can list their subscriptions, edit them, disable and enable them and create new subscriptions. In addition to managing subscriptions, it should allow for sending test events or ping events to the receiver endpoints.

Ideally, the dashboard offers a webhook event log that displays all events, the response of the webhook and the interpretation of the sender (success, failure, etc.).

4.4.3.2 Automation

An aspect of a great developer experience is helping the developer to automate development and testing capabilities around webhooks. An example is the ping endpoint, a great feature for automated integration testing: When this endpoint is called, it generates a synthetic event for testing and sends it off to the webhook (see section 5.5.3.2). The ping endpoint is usually provided as a part of the subscription API.

5 Webhook Design

Since webhooks are no standard, there are no external rules that constrain the design of webhooks, just the rules we impose ourselves. When designing webhooks for an API portfolio, we have a lot of autonomy and freedom to apply the webhooks concepts (see section 3.2) in a way that fits our needs. The other side of this freedom is the responsibility to design webhooks the right way.

In this chapter, we provide a concrete design proposal for webhooks. Each of the webhooks concepts we have introduced in chapter 3, is designed in more detail, based on the non-functional requirement introduced in chapter 4, the actual designs of well-known APIs and webhooks studied in chapter 6, and on best practice gathered in the field.

For each of the main concepts of webhooks, we discuss the main design decisions, the detailed architecture of the concept, its behavior and its interface. Each webhooks concept is also described by a specification in OpenAPI.

5.1 Webhook Description in OpenAPI

To make the concepts and designs more concrete, we provide a reference design of both the server-side and the client-side interfaces of webhooks. The design is expressed in OpenAPI 3.0, an API description language[5]. In order to learn more about API description languages, check out this book[4].

Download the Webhook Specification in OpenAPI:

https://api-university.com/books/webhooks/openapi

This design should not be understood as a dogmatic must-use. Instead, it is an illustration of the concepts introduced in this book, an inspiration and a starting point for new webhook designs. This might help you if you are an API provider, trying to add webhooks to your portfolio. Note: If you are building an API client and you want to learn how to provide webhooks for a particular, existing API (such as Stripe or BitBucket for example), then this OpenAPI spec will not help you. You need to check the details of the chosen API provider on their API portal.

5.2 Event Resource

Events are a central concept for webhooks. The core attributes of an event are its type (or topic), the time it was created and the resource that was changed.

5.2.1 Design Decisions

When designing webhooks, we need to decide how much information we want to include in an event (see sections 5.2.1.1, 5.2.1.2, 5.2.1.3) and how we want to structure the event topics (see sections 5.2.1.4).

5.2.1.1 Thick Events vs. Thin Events

Should the event contain the data of the resource that was affected by the change that triggered the event? This is an important design decision for events. And there are two alternative approaches, called thick events (see section 5.2.1.2) and thin events (see section 5.2.1.3).

5.2.1.2 Thick Events

Thick events contain as much information as possible about the event. For the receiver, thick events are practical, since all relevant information is delivered as part of the event. The downsides of thick events are (1) security concerns, (2) reliability issues and (3) stale data. Let's have a look at each of them.

(1) Security Concerns   Thick events contain the business data that is required for the receiver to act upon the event. Typically, the resource associated with the event is embedded into the event. Encryption of this data is always good, but is it absolutely required? We need to assess the data protection needs of this embedded data. Uncritical data can be included in the thick event. Critical and sensitive data either needs to be encrypted, by message encryption, by transport channel encryption or by both (see section 4.2.2.3).

(2) Reliability Issues   If the receiver relies on the business data from the event, it is essential that no events go missing, since this would result in inconsistent data. To ensure reliable event delivery, sender, and receiver need to work together and engineer a reliable delivery solution (see section 4.1). The sender needs to implement a retry mechanism (see section 4.1.4), the sender needs to record the events including their delivery status in an event history database (see section 4.1.3), and the API provider needs to provide these events via the event history API (see sections 3.2.5). This allows the client to resynchronize events that it missed despite the retry mechanism (can happen). In addition, we need to require the receiver to implement error handling according to the specification (see section 4.1.2).

(3) Stale Data Stale data can occur if events are received out of order. So first of all, we need to ensure that we can recognize the correct order of events, e.g. by providing timestamps in the event metadata. Secondly, we need to interpret the timestamps of each received event, reorder unprocessed events according to the timestamp, and discard unprocessed events if newer events have already been processed.

5.2.1.3 Thin Events

Thin events are merely notifications. They contain the metadata described in 5.2.1.1 and also the URL of the resource that was affected by the event. By retrieving the resource identified by this URL, the client can obtain the relevant business data to act upon the event. To retrieve this resource, the client has to go through the regular API, with its security mechanisms and secured transport channel.

A disadvantage of thin events is that another API call is required to get the relevant data for acting on the event. An advantage of thin events is that no additional engineering is required, to achieve security and reliability and to avoid stale data.

Event Format A common event format, which can be used by all event types, is possible for thin events. The metadata described in 5.2.1.1 is contained in every event. It also contains the URL of the resource that was affected by the event. To realize thin events in our reference design (see section 5.2.4), just ignore the attribute `Thick-Payload`.

5.2.1.4 Topics

Topics are the names we associate with the types of events. Topics are mostly used during subscription and delivery of the event.

It is best practice to form topic names of the following three parts: (1) the resource affected by the change, (2) the type of change and (3) whether the change has just started or has already completed.

(1) Since an event is typically connected to an underlying resource that changed, the resource name should be part of the topic. The client is typically familiar with the API portfolio of the API provider and the resource model represented by the API portfolio. Including the resource name into the event, helps to make the connection between the event and the affected resource. For small API portfolios, it is OK to just use the resource name, e.g. `payments`. For huge API portfolios, we need to use the full URL of the resource, since we might otherwise have naming collisions on resource names.

(2) The event is typically caused by an action or change. This is necessary if we want to distinguish between different actions that are performed on the resource. And even if no such distinctions are needed, a generic `changed` can be used as a description of the action.

(3) Sometimes it is essential to differentiate if the action has just started or has already completed. We can indicate that the action has just started by using the gerund form (`creating` or `updating`) and that the action has completed by using the past participle (`created` or `updated`).

A complete example of applying this naming convention to topics is `payment-processed`. From this topic name, it is clear that the payment resource is affected and that the event was caused because the processing-action has been completed.

5.2.1.5 Special Topics

There are three special topics that all receivers need to support in addition to the topics they actively subscribe to. These special topics are the ping topic, the confirmation topic, and the wildcard topic.

Special Topic: Ping The ping topic is used for testing a webhook. All webhooks need to be able to handle events of type ping.

Special Topic: Confirmation The confirmation topic is used during the subscription process (sent by the subscription API) to confirm that the endpoint is interested in receiving the events. All webhooks need to be able to handle events of type confirmation (see section 4.2.4.3).

Special Topic: * The wildcard topic * is a shorthand for "any supported event type."

5.2.2 Event Delivery Overview

Figure 5.1 provides a comprehensive overview of end-to-end event delivery with webhooks. It is a more detailed version of figure 3.3 on page 41.

The server-side application places raw events into the event queue after they have occurred in the application (1). Asynchronously, the event sender controller (see section 5.3.2.1) takes raw events out of the raw event queue (2), finds matching subscriptions and hands the event data structure to the next available worker (3). The assigned event sender worker (see section 5.3.2.1) transforms the raw events into an individual event data

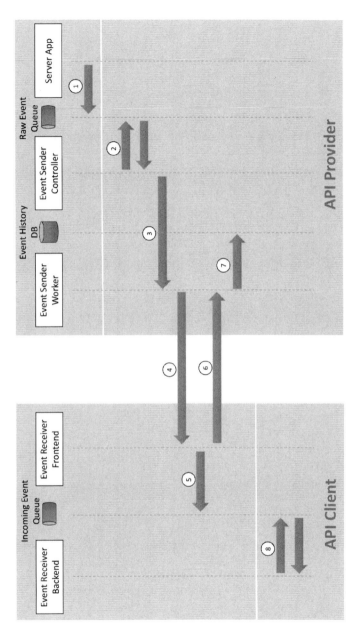

Figure 5.1: Event Delivery Overview

structure targeted for the receiver including its credentials and signature, and (4) sends the event data structure as a request to the event receiver endpoint (see section 5.4). The assigned worker waits for the response, while the event receiver frontend (see section 5.4.2.1) takes the incoming events (4), validates the content, such as the security token or signature, and puts them into a sorted priority queue (5). The frontend synchronously sends off the response to the sender (6) before the event has been processed by the event receiver backend. The assigned sender worker gets the response (6) from the event receiver. The response may be a success, a failure or a timeout. The worker reports both the event and the response in the event history database (7). Asynchronously, the event receiver backend (see section 5.4.2.2) reads the next event from the priority queue and processes it (8).

If you are interested in a more detailed description of the event delivery, check section 5.3.3 for a detailed description of what happens on the provider-side and section 5.4.3 for a detailed description of what happens on the client-side.

5.2.3 Attributes

Events consist of the following attributes:

- ID, a UUID that identifies this event instance

- Topic, type of event as described in section 5.2.1.4

- Latest-Delivery, timestamp of the latest delivery attempt

- First-Delivery, timestamp of the first delivery attempt

- Delivery-Attempt, number of times this event has been attempted to be delivered

- `Delivery-State`, indicates whether the event has been delivered

- `Subscription-ID`, a UUID that identifies the subscription based on which this event is delivered; this ID is used for managing the subscription, such as unsubscribing

- `Affected-Resource`, URL of the resource affected by the change, this attribute is essential for thin events (see section 5.2.1.3)

- `Thick-Payload`, optionally the content of the changed resource, this attribute is only used for thick events (see section 5.2.1.2)

5.2.4 OpenAPI Specification

Here is an excerpt from the OpenAPI specification of the event resource. Note, that you cannot use this excerpt in isolation, but only together with the excerpts of other webhooks concepts. If you want to use this specification, you do not need to type this! Download the complete webhooks specification code at
http://api-university.com/books/webhooks/openapi

```
openapi: 3.0.0
info:
  description: API Portfolio with Webhook Management Endpoints
  version: "1.0.0"
  title: API Portfolio with Webhook Management Endpoints
  contact:
    email: matt@api-university.com
  license:
    name: Apache 2.0
    url: 'http://www.apache.org/licenses/LICENSE-2.0.html'
components:
  schemas:
    Event:
      type: object
      required:
        - id
        - topic
        - latest-delivery
        - first-delivery
        - delivery-attempt
        - delivery-state
        - subscription-id
        - affected-resource
```

```
    properties:
      id:
        description: identifies this event
        type: string
        format: uuid
        example: 4f90f1ee-6c54-4b01-90e6-d701748f08534
      topic:
        description: indicates what type of event occurred
        type: string
        example: 'https://api.mydomain.com/email-sent'
      latest-delivery:
        description: timestamp of the latest delivery attempt
        type: string
        format: date-time
        example: '2017-08-29T09:12:33.001Z'
      first-delivery:
        description: timestamp of the first delivery attempt
        type: string
        format: date-time
        example: '2017-08-29T09:10:32.001Z'
      delivery-attempt:
        description: number of times this event has been attempted to be delivered
        type: integer
        example: 2
      delivery-state:
        description: indicates whether the event has been delivered
        type: string
        enum:
          - 'delivered'
          - 'open'
        default: 'open'
        example: 'open'
      subscription-id:
        description: |
          Identifies the subscription.
          This ID is used for managing the subscription,
          such as unsubscribing.
        type: string
        format: uuid
        example: d290f1ee-6c54-4b01-90e6-d701748f0851
      affected-resource:
        description: URL of the resource affected by the change
        type: string
        format: url
        example: 'https://api.mydomain.com/email/1234'
      thick-payload:
        description: OPTIONAL - payload of the changed resource
        type: string
        example: |
          '{
            "to": "john@company.com",
            "subject": "Your speech",
            "body": "Thanks for your speech yesterday. Excellent."
          }'
```

5.3 Event Sender

The event sender's task is to observe all internal changes, determine if any subscriber is interested in receiving the observed

change, create event messages for the observed events and send the event messages to the respective receiver endpoints. The event sender uses the event resource (see section 5.2) as its data structure for sending event messages.

5.3.1 Design Decisions

5.3.1.1 Performance and Scalability

To deal with high load on the server side, the sender should be scalable. To achieve this, we decompose the sender into a controller and some stateless sender workers (see section 4.3.2). A sender worker is responsible for sending an event request and reporting the response. The controller is responsible for assigning events to workers and initiating the retry mechanism, so we avoid coupling a long-running retry logic to a sender worker.

5.3.1.2 Reliability

Ensuring reliability is, of course, the responsibility of both sender and receiver. But the sender needs to do the heavy lifting. It is the sender's task to recognizing event delivery errors (see section 4.1.2), keep an event history (see section 4.1.3), and manage the retry mechanism (see section 4.1.4).

5.3.1.3 Security

For a more comprehensive treatment of security on the event sender endpoint, check out section 4.2.2. In the following, we provide just a brief summary.

The sender does not offer a publicly available service that others can connect to and that needs to be secured. Security in the context of the event sender is all about satisfying the security demands of the receiver.

The sender needs to authenticate the receiver, and it needs to make sure, that the receiver can authenticate the sender, by supporting the authentication mechanisms (see section 4.2.1).

5.3.2 Architecture

The sender consists of a number of components, as shown in figure 5.2: a *controller* (see section 5.3.2.1) that collects events and prepares them for the subscribers and a number of stateless sender *workers* (see section 5.3.2.2) which actually deliver the events to the clients and report the delivery state. There are two data storages to support the sender: the *raw event queue* (see section 5.3.2.3) with raw events that have just occurred and wait to be prepared for sending and the *event history database* (see section 5.3.2.4), which keeps a record of all the events and their delivery state.

In figure 5.2 you can also see the surrounding systems of the event sender that it needs to interact with: The server app produces the raw events and places them into the raw event queue. There is a number of receivers that the sender needs to send events to. The sender records the events and their respective delivery status in an event history database. The sender also needs to have access to the subscription database, to figure out which event type to send to which event receiver.

5.3.2.1 Event Sender Controller

The controller is responsible for preparing raw events, finding relevant subscriptions in the subscription database, transforming the raw events into event messages that can be sent out, assigning events to available workers, and initiating the retry mechanism when necessary.

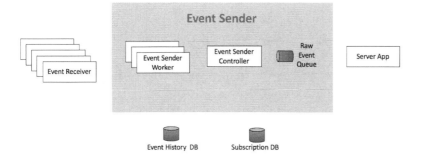

Figure 5.2: Event Sender Architecture

5.3.2.2 Event Sender Worker

A sender worker is responsible for sending an event request, waiting for the response, and report the response in the event history database.

5.3.2.3 Raw Event Queue

The server-side application places raw events into the event queue after they have occurred in the application. The controller takes raw events out of the event queue and determines for each raw event if a matching subscription exists. The controller can perform this work asynchronously, as soon as it has the necessary capacity. The event queue decouples the server application from the controller.

5.3.2.4 Event History Database

The event history database is a record of all the events that have been attempted to be delivered. The workers write the events including the delivery status into the event history database.

5.3.3 Behavior

When designing an event sender, it is important that the event sender has a high event throughput. This is why its components need to work well together. The interactions between the components are visualized in figure 5.3.

This is only a part of the end-to-end event delivery: check out figure 5.1 on page 71 and section 5.2.2 for a comprehensive overview of event delivery.

The server-side application places raw events into the raw event queue after they have occurred in the application (1). This operation is relatively quick and reliable and should not affect the performance of the server app.

Asynchronously, when the controller has the capacity, it takes raw events out of the raw event queue (2) and determines for each raw event if a matching subscription exists, based on information from the subscription database. If there are multiple pending events for the same subscription, the controller may choose to *batch* the events, i.e. send all of the events together as a bundle in one event data structure. The controller hands the event data structure to the next available worker (3).

The assigned worker sends the event data structure as a request to the receiver endpoint (4). But before it can do that, it personalizes the event data structure for just that receiver, based on information from the subscription database. The worker uses the correct credentials for authentication with that particular receiver and signs the payload with the shared secret for that particular receiver.

The assigned worker waits for the response (6) from the event receiver. The response may be a success, a failure or a timeout. The worker reports both the event and the response in the event history database (7).

The controller also manages the retry mechanism, based on the data from the event history database. For details about the

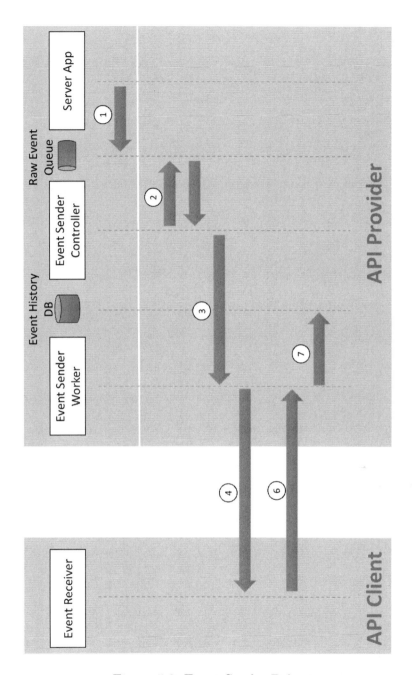

Figure 5.3: Event Sender Behavior

retry mechanism, check out section 4.1.4.

5.4 Event Receiver

The event receiver endpoint (or webhook) receives and processes events on the client side. It expects the incoming events in the form of an event resource (see section 5.2).

An event receiver is implemented by the API consumer. The API provider only hands out a detailed specification for implementation of the event receiver and the API consumer implements it. This specification includes both a description of the interface and a description of the expected observable behavior.

5.4.1 Design Decisions

5.4.1.1 Idempotence

The receiver endpoint needs to be idempotent, since the sender may resend the same event e.g. due to the retry mechanism. In our context, the meaning of idempotence is that the effect of sending the event multiple times is the same as sending the event only once.

5.4.1.2 Security

For a more comprehensive treatment of security on the event receiver endpoint, check out section 4.2.1. In the following, we provide just a summary.

The sender needs to be authenticated (see section 4.2.1.1) by verifying the username and password or the client certificate. The message authenticity (see section 4.2.1.2) needs to be verified by recomputing the signature and comparing the computed signature against the signature received with the request.

A part of ensuring the security is also validating the schema conformance of the incoming events (see section 5.2.4). Also, the timestamp (see section 4.2.1.3) in the event message needs to be checked and compared to the current time to prevent replay attacks. The IP of the sender should be whitelisted (see section 4.2.1.5), traffic from other IPs should be blocked. The URL of the receiver endpoint should be kept a secret (see section 4.2.1.5), and it should be chosen to contain a random string, so it cannot be easily guessed.

5.4.1.3 Availability

The event receiver needs to be highly available and capable of handling large amounts of incoming events, without getting flooded. By minimizing the response time of the receiver and processing events asynchronously, we can prevent event flooding (see section 4.3.1) and ensure high availability of the receiver endpoint.

5.4.1.4 Support Testing and Pinging

The event receiver needs to support testing and ping events, which are sent for testing purposes. In fact, the client can use the so-called ping endpoint (see section 5.5.3.2) of the subscription API to send a ping event to the receiver endpoint. The events are of type `ping` (see section 5.2.1.5), which the receiver needs to support.

5.4.1.5 Support Confirmation

During the subscription process, a confirmation is sent to the receiver endpoint. The confirmation is sent as an event of type `confirmation`. The receiver needs to support confirmation events and process them (see section 4.2.4.3) by validating the subscription and returning the challenge.

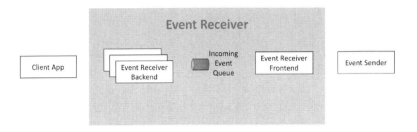

Figure 5.4: Event Receiver Architecture

5.4.2 Architecture

The event receiver needs to be highly available and capable of handling large amounts of incoming events. To minimize the response time of the receiver, incoming events are not processed synchronously. Incoming events are validated and then queued, so that a response can be returned immediately to the event sender. The stored events can be processed asynchronously.

As shown in figure 5.4, an event receiver consists of a frontend component (see section 5.4.2.1), several instances of backend components (see section 5.4.2.2) and an incoming event queue (see section 5.4.2.3).

The event receiver works with other components, such as the event sender and also very closely with the client app. The event receiver is actually a part of the client app, where its task is to trigger internal actions that realize business functionality.

5.4.2.1 Event Receiver Frontend

The frontend takes the incoming events, validates their content, such as the security token or signature, and puts them into a sorted priority queue for asynchronous processing. Then the receiver sends a response back to the sender.

5.4.2.2 Event Receiver Backend

The backend reads events from the priority queue and processes them. The event processing is specific to the client application.

5.4.2.3 Incoming Event Queue

The incoming event queue is a priority queue, which sorts the events it holds according to the timestamp (it is an attribute of the event).

5.4.3 Behavior

The main task of the event receiver (or webhook) is to receive and process incoming events (see section 5.4.3.1). Sporadically, the event receiver needs to perform the task of subscription confirmation (see section 5.4.3.2), initially during the event subscription and then periodically in the form of a subscription reconfirmation.

5.4.3.1 Event Handling

Figure 5.5 visualizes the interactions for receiving events. This is only a part of the end-to-end event delivery: check out figure 5.1 on page 71 and section 5.2.2 for a comprehensive overview of event delivery.

The frontend takes the incoming events (4), validates the content, such as their security token or signature, and puts them into a sorted priority queue (5). Events may arrive out of order e.g. due to network delays. Since the events should be processed to avoid stale data, the frontend attempts to sort the events before they get processed. The frontend synchronously sends off the response (6) before the event was internally processed. A positive response is sent with a 202 Accepted HTTP status code. A negative response is sent with a 4xx HTTP status

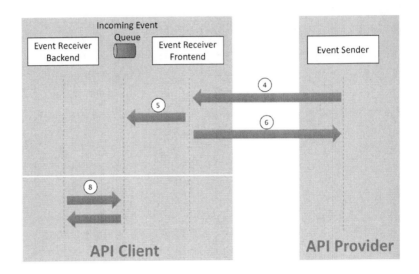

Figure 5.5: Event Receiver Behavior

code, e.g. a 400 Bad Request if the input was not understood, a 404 Not Found if the given event topic is not handled by this webhook, a 401 Unauthorized if the client cannot be authenticated, or a 403 Forbidden if the signature does not match.

The backend reads events from the incoming event queue and processes them (8). The event processing is specific to the client application. Sometimes out-of-order-events may slip through the sorting of the frontend component and the priority queue. This is not necessarily an issue and only needs to be addressed if thick events (see section 5.2.1.2) are used and if the out-of-order event has a timestamp that is before an already processed event that refers to the same resource.

5.4.3.2 Subscription Confirmation

The event receiver needs to support subscription confirmation as described in section 4.2.4.3. The request contains the subscription attributes and a challenge value, a random value generated by the server, which needs to be returned to the server to confirm the subscription.

The confirmation request comes in as a regular event of type `confirmation` (see section 5.2.1.5). In the payload part of the event, the subscription configuration is contained. This subscription configuration needs to be extracted, parsed and validated. If the outcome of subscription validation is positive, the challenge attribute needs to be extracted from the event and the value of the challenge needs to be returned in the body of the response to complete the subscription confirmation.

5.4.4 Interface

The event receiver has one endpoint which is also called webhook endpoint. It can be accessed via the POST HTTP method.

- `POST /webhooks/{webhook-name}` The receiver endpoint. The sender uses the POST method to send its events here. The path parameter `webhook-name` is to be chosen according to the guidelines specified in section 4.2.1.5.

5.4.5 OpenAPI Specification

Note: The OpenAPI Spec for the event receiver does not contain the security scheme for authentication, simply because multiple security schemes are possible (e.g. HTTP Basic Auth, HTTPS Client Certificate).

Here is an excerpt from the OpenAPI specification of the event receiver. Note, that you cannot use this excerpt in isolation, but only together with the excerpts of other webhooks concepts. If you want to use this, you do not need to type this! Download the complete webhooks specification code at

http://api-university.com/books/webhooks/openapi

```
openapi: 3.0.0
info:
  description: Client-Side Webhook Endpoints
  version: "1.0.0"
  title: Client-Side Webhook Endpoints
  contact:
    email: matt@api-university.com
  license:
    name: Apache 2.0
    url: 'http://www.apache.org/licenses/LICENSE-2.0.html'
paths:
  /webhooks/{webhook-name}:
    post:
      summary: Webhook, to be implemented on the client-side.
      description: Webhook, to be implemented on the client-side.
      parameters:
        - in: header
          name: Signature
          description: signature of the body
          required: true
          schema:
            type: string
      requestBody:
        content:
          application/json:
            schema:
              $ref: '#/components/schemas/Event'
        description: Subscription to be confirmed
      responses:
        '202':
          description: Accepted the event for asynchronous processing.
        '400':
          description: Invalid Event received.
        '401':
          description: Unauthorized.
        '403':
          description: Signature mismatch.
        '404':
          description: Webhook not found or topic not processed here.
        '500':
          description: Server error, try again later.
        '503':
          description: Server error, server is overloaded, try again later.
```

5.5 Subscription API

The event subscription API is used for managing the subscriptions of the authenticated client. The client can retrieve a list of all active subscriptions, create a new subscription, retrieve the details of an existing subscription, delete a subscription or change the attributes of an existing subscription. The subscription API uses the subscription resource (see section 5.6) as its data structure.

5.5.1 Design Decisions

5.5.1.1 Mountpoint

What is the place of the subscription API in the API portfolio? Or, to speak with a Unix analogy, where do we mount the subscription API in the API portfolio? The subscription API should be a top-level resource in the API portfolio.

5.5.1.2 Subscription Reconfirmation

Unused webhooks may accumulate. Thus it is a good idea to reconfirm subscriptions regularly using the algorithm described in section 4.2.4.3. If the reconfirmation fails, the subscription expires. Once set up, reconfirmation can be scheduled automatically.

5.5.1.3 Ping and Test Endpoints

To test the webhook associated with a subscription via API call, a ping or test endpoint may be designed. Based on the given subscription resource a matching test event can be generated and sent to the receiver endpoint of the subscription.

5.5.1.4 Topics Endpoint

A topic endpoint delivers the static list of topics, which are supported by the API provider, in a machine-readable form.

5.5.2 Architecture

The API is a CRUD interface to the subscription resource (see section 5.6). Its data is held in the subscription database. So from an architectural perspective, this API is not very complex.

5.5.3 Behavior

The client can retrieve a list of all active subscriptions, create a new subscription, retrieve the details of an existing subscription, delete a subscription or change a subscription.

5.5.3.1 Subscription Confirmation

When changes (POST, PUT, DELETE) on subscription resources are requested, they need to be confirmed by the client. This is supposed to mitigate that an attacker can register an unsuspecting endpoint for receiving events.

The necessary interaction between the subscription API and the receiver endpoint of the client are visualized in figure 5.6. Every time the subscription is changed via the API (1), the subscription change needs to be confirmed by the receiver endpoint (2), and the change is only executed if the receiver endpoint confirms (3). Then the response of the subscription API is sent back to the client (4).

To perform the confirmation, the subscription API needs to prepare the confirmation event (2), which is a regular event with topic `confirmation` (see section 5.2.1.5). The payload part of the confirmation event contains the new or changed subscription configuration and a challenge value. The challenge value is randomly generated on the side of the API provider.

The webhook is supposed to validate the subscription and return the challenge value in the body part of the response (3). If the challenge value is correct, the change can be executed, and the subscription operation succeeds (4).

5.5.3.2 Ping Endpoint

We have defined a ping endpoint as a subresource for every subscription. When a client calls the ping endpoint, a ping event (see section 5.2.1.5) is created on the server and sent to the

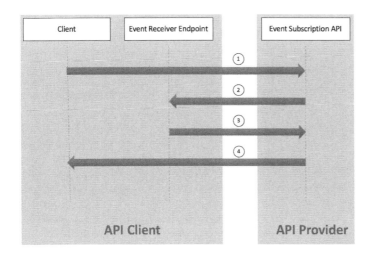

Figure 5.6: Subscription Behavior

associated webhook. This is a great feature for automated integration testing.

Note: The ping endpoint is protected with OAuth Client Credentials[7], so it can only be called by the client.

5.5.4 Interface

When webhooks are used for RESTful APIs, then webhook subscription management should also be RESTful. The subscription API offers the basic operations on the subscription resource (see section 5.6), a subresource for sending ping events, and a subresource for listing the available topics.

- GET /subscriptions, lists the available subscriptions that are currently set up for the authenticated client.

- POST /subscriptions, creates a new subscription resource and returns the URL of the newly created subscription resource in the Location HTTP header of the response if all validations and confirmations are successful.

- GET /subscriptions/{id}, returns a specific subscription resource with the given id.

- DELETE /subscriptions/{id}, unsubscribes from the subscription with the given id.

- PUT /subscriptions/{id}, updates a specific subscription resource with the given id.

- POST /subscriptions/{id}/ping, sends a ping event to the webhook of this subscription.

- GET /subscriptions/topics, lists the available event types via API.

5.5.5 OpenAPI Specification

Here is an excerpt from the OpenAPI specification of the subscription API. Note, that you cannot use this excerpt in isolation, but only together with the excerpts of other webhooks concepts. If you want to use this specification, you do not need to type this! Download the complete webhooks specification code at

http://api-university.com/books/webhooks/openapi

```
openapi: 3.0.0
info:
  description: API Portfolio with Webhook Management Endpoints
  version: "1.0.0"
  title: API Portfolio with Webhook Management Endpoints
  contact:
    email: matt@api-university.com
  license:
    name: Apache 2.0
    url: 'http://www.apache.org/licenses/LICENSE-2.0.html'
paths:
  /subscriptions:
    get:
      summary: Lists available subscriptions
      description: Lists the available subscriptions for the authenticated client.
      responses:
```

```yaml
        '200':
          description: available subscriptions
          content:
            application/json:
              schema:
                type: array
                items:
                  $ref: '#/components/schemas/Subscription'
      security:
        - oauth-client-credentials: []
    post:
      summary: Creates a subscription
      description: |
        Create a new subscription configuration and returns the URL
        of the newly created subscription resource in the Location HTTP Header
        of the response if all validations and confirmations are successful.
      responses:
        '201':
          description: subscription created
        '400':
          description: 'invalid input, object invalid'
        '409':
          description: an existing item already exists
      requestBody:
        content:
          application/json:
            schema:
              $ref: '#/components/schemas/Subscription'
        description: subscription to be added
      security:
        - oauth-client-credentials: []
  /subscriptions/{id}:
    parameters:
      - in: path
        name: id
        description: id of the subscription
        required: true
        schema:
          type: string
    get:
      summary: Read the respective subscription
      description: Returns a specific subscription resource with the given id.
      responses:
        '200':
          description: subscription configuration
          content:
            application/json:
              schema:
                $ref: '#/components/schemas/Subscription'
        '404':
          description: not found
      security:
        - oauth-client-credentials: []
    delete:
      summary: Unsubscribes
      description: Unsubscribes from the subscription with the given id.
      responses:
        '200':
          description: deleted
        '404':
          description: not found
      security:
        - oauth-client-credentials: []
    put:
      summary: Updates the respective subscription
```

```
            description: Updates a specific subscription resource with the given id.
            responses:
              '200':
                description: subscription updated
              '400':
                description: 'invalid input, object invalid'
              '404':
                description: not found
            requestBody:
              content:
                application/json:
                  schema:
                    $ref: '#/components/schemas/Subscription'
              description: the updated subscription
            security:
              - oauth-client-credentials: []
  /subscriptions/{id}/ping:
    parameters:
      - in: path
        name: id
        description: id of the subscription
        required: true
        schema:
          type: string
    post:
      summary: Sends a ping event to the webhook
      description: |
        Simulates an event being triggered.
        Sends a sample event to the webhook of this subscription.
      responses:
        '200':
          description: ping scheduled
      security:
        - oauth-client-credentials: []
  /subscriptions/topics:
    get:
      summary: Lists available topics
      description: |
        Lists the available event types via API.
        This API is open to unauthenticated clients
        and can be called anonymously.
      responses:
        '200':
          description: |
            Just a static list of topics
            that can be subscribed to
            with this subscriptions endpoint
          content:
            application/json:
              schema:
                type: array
                items:
                  type: string
securitySchemes:
  oauth-client-credentials:
    type: oauth2
    flows:
      clientCredentials:
        tokenUrl: https://api.mydomain.com/oauth/token
```

5.6 Subscription Resource

A subscription can be seen as a contract between API client and API provider. In this contract, the provider agrees to send a certain type of event, and the client agrees to have a highly available webhook endpoint that can receive these types of event. The technical details of this contract are described in the subscription resource, which is sometimes also called subscription configuration or subscription contract.

The subscription resource is exposed via the subscription API (see section 5.5), which provides CRUD operations to authorized clients. Only the client that created the respective resource is allowed to access it.

5.6.1 Attributes

A subscription resource contains the following attributes:

- ID, the UUID of the subscription

- Webhook, the URL of the receiver (= webhook)

- Topics, the types of events we want to be notified about, an array of strings.

- Filter, limits the events which should be notified on to events that match this filter, typically the filter is applied on an attribute of the affected resource, the detailed semantics needs to be defined in a domain-specific way.

- Active, with this flag a subscription can be temporarily deactivated

- Signing-Secret, shared secret to be used for signing the events

- `Authentication-Mechanism`, mechanism used for protecting the receiver

- `Authentication-ID`, username to be used by the sender for authentication, if any

- `Authentication-Secret`, password to be used by the sender for authentication, if any

- `Confirmation`, timestamp of the most recent (re)confirmation of the receiver endpoint

5.6.2 OpenAPI Specification

Here is an excerpt from the OpenAPI specification of the Subscription Resource. Note, that you cannot use this excerpt in isolation, but only together with the excerpts of the other webhooks concepts. If you want to use this specification, you do not need to type this! Download the complete webhooks specification code at

http://api-university.com/books/webhooks/openapi

```
openapi: 3.0.0
info:
  description: API Portfolio with Webhook Management Endpoints
  version: "1.0.0"
  title: API Portfolio with Webhook Management Endpoints
  contact:
    email: matt@api-university.com
  license:
    name: Apache 2.0
    url: 'http://www.apache.org/licenses/LICENSE-2.0.html'
components:
  schemas:
    Subscription:
      type: object
      required:
        - id
        - webhook
        - topics
        - filter
        - active
        - authentication-mechanism
        - confirmation
      properties:
        id:
          description: ID of the subscription
          type: string
```

```
        format: uuid
        example: d290f1ee-6c54-4b01-90e6-d701748f0851
webhook:
        description: the URL of the receiver (= webhook)
        type: string
        format: url
        example: 'http://my-client.com/webhook/f673h8db'
topics:
        description: the types of events we want to be notified about
        type: array
        items:
          type: string
        example: ['https://api.mydomain.com/email-sent']
filter:
        description: |
          only consider events that match this filter,
          typically it is something domain specific
        type: string
        example: 'sender:matt@api-university.com'
active:
        description: only for active subscriptions events are delivered
        type: boolean
        default: true
        example: true
signing-secret:
        description: shared secret to be used for signing the events
        type: string
        example: 'ksadf9872h3rnkwfeiu4nds9723k2ciw89'
authentication-mechanism:
        description: mechanism used for protecting the receiver
        type: string
        enum:
          - 'Basic'
          - 'Certificate'
        default: 'Basic'
        example: ' Basic'
authentication-id:
        description: |
          OPTIONAL - username
          to be used for sender authentication, if any
        type: string
        example: 'my-client'
authentication-secret:
        description: |
          OPTIONAL - password
          to be used for sender authentication, if any
        type: string
        example: 'my-secret'
confirmation:
        description: |
          indicates the point in time of
          the most recent (re)confirmation
          of the receiver endpoint
        type: string
        format: date-time
        example: '2017-08-29T09:12:33.001Z'
```

5.7 Event History API

When the receiver endpoint is down for some time, it cannot receive events during the downtime. Are all these events lost? Not if the API provider offers an event history API.

Clients can use the event history API for manual reconciliation. The event history API gives clients access to all the events that could not be delivered. Based on this data, clients can process undelivered events in a batch operation.

The event history API provides access to the *event history database* (see section 5.3.2.4), which keeps records of all the events that have been attempted to be delivered, including their delivery state. The event history API uses the event resource (see section 5.2) as its data structure.

5.7.1 Behavior

The event history API is protected, clients are authenticated, and access is limited to the event history of the authenticated client. When manual resynchronization needs to be performed, the API can be used to retrieve all the events that have not been able to be delivered. When an event has gotten manually synchronized, its delivery state can be updated via the API.

The API allows for reading and updating events. Updating the resource may be limited to updating the delivery-status attribute. The API does not allow for creating or deleting events.

When retrieving event listings, large amounts of data may be returned. The client can instruct the API to filter the list of events (e.g. by topic, data, delivery status) and thus have it return only selected events.

5.7.2 Interface

- GET /events, lists recent events from the event history of the authenticated client. You can limit the number of events that are returned with any combination of the following optional query parameters:
    - limit: maximum number of events
    - topic: filter events by the given topic
    - after: only select events that have occurred after the given time
    - delivery-state: only select events that have a certain delivery state, e.g. only events that have not been delivered yet.

- GET /events/{id}, reads the event with the given id from the event history if the event is supposed to be delivered to the authenticated client.

- PUT /events/{id}, updates the event with the given id in the event history if the event is supposed to be delivered to the authenticated client. The only thing that can be updated is the delivery-state attribute.

5.7.3 OpenAPI Specification

Here is the OpenAPI specification of the event history API. Note, that there are dependencies, e.g. to the event resource (see section 5.2.4). If you want to use this specification, you do not need to type this! Download the complete webhooks specification code at

http://api-university.com/books/webhooks/openapi

```
openapi: 3.0.0
info:
  description: API Portfolio with Webhook Management Endpoints
  version: "1.0.0"
  title: API Portfolio with Webhook Management Endpoints
```

```yaml
  contact:
    email: matt@api-university.com
  license:
    name: Apache 2.0
    url: 'http://www.apache.org/licenses/LICENSE-2.0.html'
paths:
  /events:
    get:
      summary: Lists recent events
      description: |
        Lists recent events from the event history
        of the authenticated client.
      parameters:
        - in: query
          name: limit
          description: |
            OPTIONAL - maximum number of most
            recent events that should be returned
          required: false
          schema:
            type: string
        - in: query
          name: topic
          description: |
            OPTIONAL - filter events by the given topic
          required: false
          schema:
            type: string
        - in: query
          name: delivery-state
          description: |
            OPTIONAL - only select events
            that have a certain delivery-state
          required: false
          schema:
            type: string
        - in: query
          name: after
          description: |
            OPTIONAL - only select events that have occured
            after the given time
          required: false
          schema:
            type: string
            format: date-time
            example: '2017-08-29T09:12:33.001Z'
      responses:
        '200':
          description: recent events of the authenticated client
          content:
            application/json:
              schema:
                type: array
                items:
                  $ref: '#/components/schemas/Event'
      security:
        - oauth-client-credentials: []
  /events/{id}:
    parameters:
      - in: path
        name: id
        description: id of the event
        required: true
        schema:
          type: string
```

```yaml
    get:
      summary: Reads the respective event from the event history
      description: |
        Reads the event with the given id from the event history,
        if the event is supposed to be delivered to the authenticated client.
      responses:
        '200':
          description: event
          content:
            application/json:
              schema:
                $ref: '#/components/schemas/Event'
        '404':
          description: not found
      security:
      - oauth-client-credentials: []
    put:
      summary: Updates the respective event in the event history
      description: |
        Updates the event with the given id in the event history,
        if the event is supposed to be delivered to the authenticated client.
        The only thing that can be updated in the state attribute.
      responses:
        '200':
          description: event updated
        '400':
          description: 'invalid input, object invalid'
        '404':
          description: not found
      requestBody:
        content:
          application/json:
            schema:
              $ref: '#/components/schemas/Event'
        description: the updated event
      security:
      - oauth-client-credentials: []
securitySchemes:
  oauth-client-credentials:
    type: oauth2
    flows:
      clientCredentials:
        tokenUrl: https://api.mydomain.com/oauth/token
```

6 Webhooks in the Wild

When designing webhooks for a particular app, I recommend studying the webhook designs of well-known API providers to learn and get inspired. We study the webhooks provided by apps in different business domains an as we will see, the webhooks of these apps are designed to support the essential characteristics of the app.

The webhooks of an instant messaging app (see section 6.2), need to be very tough on enforcing timing constraints, so the app maintains its instant, fast and responsive character. Receiver endpoints need to react within a few seconds, retries are only attempted a small number of times and only happen within minutes. Old events are neither archived nor made accessible via API, since the value of old events diminishes quickly in the world of instant messaging.

The webhooks of a payment processing app (see section 6.3), focus on another set of properties. Here webhooks need to enforce reliability and security. Events are signed with a secure message authentication algorithm, receiver endpoints are encouraged to use HTTPS and may be protected by HTTP Basic Auth, all events are archived for later retrieval, and retries are performed hourly for several days.

Let's have a look at the webhook designs of Intercom (section 6.1), Slack (section 6.2), Stripe (section 6.3), BitBucket (section 6.4) and GitHub (section 6.5).

6.1 Intercom

Intercom is a customer engagement service; it is well known for the little chat window that pops up on websites to engage with visitors. It might be for marketing, sales or customer support. Intercom offers webhooks to allow client applications to receive notifications, such as conversation replies or new user accounts being created.

To get familiar with the details, check out the Intercom webhooks tutorial on

https://docs.intercom.com/integrations/webhooks

and the Intercom API reference documentation on

https://developers.intercom.com/v2.0/reference

6.1.1 Events

Intercom uses *thick events* (see section 5.2.1.1), so events contain relevant data as payload. This event payload is actually the same data structure that is used to deliver resources via API calls.

There are a number of predefined event types, and also a wildcard event type, which allows subscribing to all predefined event types. Intercom also allows clients, to create their own custom event types and to register webhooks for them.

6.1.2 Event Receiver Endpoint

Event receivers are, of course, required to support the event types that they are subscribed to. In addition, all event receivers need to support the ping event type (see section 5.5.3.2), even if it has not explicitly subscribed to.

6.1.3 Event History API

Intercom webhooks offer clients access to their event history. The event history is modeled as a part of the subscription API.

There are two filter configurations available for the event history: (1) an `error` feed returning a list of recent events that failed to deliver and (2) a `sent` feed returning a list of all recently sent events.

6.1.4 Subscription API

Clients can use either the subscription API or a webhook dashboard (see section 3.2.6) to subscribe to events. The interactions around the subscription API works as described in section 3.3.2, except that no subscription confirmation is expected from the receiver endpoint. The number of subscriptions per client is limited, a maximum of 250 subscriptions are allowed for each client.

6.1.5 Non-Functional Properties

6.1.5.1 Security

Intercom uses OAuth to protect its APIs, such as the event history API and the subscription API.

Receiver endpoints can be integrated via HTTPS or HTTP. Calls to the receiver endpoint are not authenticated.

Message authentication is offered as an optional feature, it can be switched on or off. The signature is computed with the HMAC SHA-1 algorithm and is transported in the `X-Hub-Signature` HTTP header.

6.1.5.2 Developer Experience

Intercom offers an API portal with documentation and a dashboard for managing webhooks. Noteworthy is an interesting feature for testing webhooks: a ping event can be sent programmatically to the webhook via a ping endpoint (offered as a sub-resource on the subscription API). The ping endpoint allows the client to trigger a test case. It is a great productivity tool for developers and an essential feature for automated integration testing.

6.2 Slack

Slack is an instant messaging application, which has lots of third-party integrations. It offers various APIs, such as a web API, a real-time-messaging API and an events API. The events API offers webhook management. To learn more, check out the Slack webhooks tutorial on

   https://api.slack.com/events-api

6.2.1 Events

Slack support a long list of events, grouped into team events and bot events. Events correspond to resources. Events are triggered e.g. when a new chat message is posted when a new team member joins etc.

6.2.2 Event Receiver Endpoint

A client application can only have one event receiver. This means that the client needs to perform the dispatching or routing depending on the event type, after event data has been received.

   The sender limits the rate of outgoing traffic for each client to 5000 events/hour, allowing for bursts of up to 2000 events. This allows the receiver to predict maximum load that can hit the endpoint. This is important because Slack is very strict on the performance of the receiver, and wants receivers to respond within 3 seconds, otherwise, it throws a timeout.

   Slack proposes to put events into a queue as soon as they have been received on the endpoint and handle them asynchronously, as proposed in section 5.4. Slack does not batch multiple events into one request, but always sends one events per request.

6.2.3 Event Sender

The sender has a short timeout of 3 seconds, follows 2 HTTP redirects when a 3xx status code is returned from the receiver and eventually, after a maximum of 2 redirects, it expects a 2xx HTTP status code.

Slack considers event delivery to have failed if (1) it is unable to negotiate or validate the SSL certificate of the client (2), the timeout of 3 seconds has exceeded, or (3) no 2xx HTTP status code has been received in the response after the 2 redirects.

The event sender of Slack uses a retry mechanism. Event delivery are retried 3 times, with an exponential back-off strategy (immediately, after 1 minute, after 5 minutes). In the HTTP header, it sends the number of retries and the reason for the retry.

When the client produces 500 failure conditions in a 30 min time window, all subscriptions of the client are disabled and an email alert is sent to the registered developer.

6.2.4 Subscription API

The subscription API is similar to the one designed in section 5.5 and even employs a confirmation with a challenge.

6.2.5 Event History API

Slack is used for instant messaging, its value is mainly provided by the communication in real-time. The value of an old message that arrives after several hours is quite low. This is probably why slack does not seem to offer an event history API.

6.2.6 Non-Functional Properties

6.2.6.1 Security

In order to be allowed to subscribe to a certain event, an OAuth scope [7, 3] matching the event is required.

6.2.6.2 Developer Experience

Clients can subscribe to an event via the webhook dashboard (see section 3.2.6) or via the subscription API.

6.3 Stripe

Stripe offers an API to create custom payment flows. And in order to build custom payment flows, it allows clients to receive events such as a successful charge or a failed charge via webhooks. To learn more, check out the Stripe webhooks tutorial on

https://stripe.com/docs/webhooks

and the API reference documentation on

https://stripe.com/docs/api#events

6.3.1 Events

Stipe offers events for a successful charge or a failed charge, which allows clients to keep their records up-to-date, send some marketing based on the customer's behavior, update a customer's membership record in the application database when a subscription payment succeeds, email a customer when a subscription payment fails or log an accounting entry when a transfer is paid. Stripe uses thin events (see section 5.2.1.1) and sensitive information is never included in a webhook event.

6.3.2 Event Receiver Endpoint

Stripe provides a guideline for webhook implementation. The expected status codes are described and the expectations for HTTPs are clearly explained.

Stripe offers a retry mechanism, which retries once an hour for up to 3 days. This is one of the longer retry timeframes, but then it is also some important payment data that is communicated via Stripe events. Due to the retry mechanism, the same request may be sent more than once. Thus Stripe advocates that receiver endpoints are idempotent.

A receiver endpoint may be protected by a HTTP basic authentication. Stripe offers to configure username password for each receiver endpoint and the sender endpoint handles the proper authentication via HTTP basic.

6.3.3 Event History API

Stripe offers an event history API for manual reconciliation. Stripe offers this possibility since important payment data is communicated via Stripe APIs and Stripe events. The events history API of Stripe list all events going back up to 30 days. Similar as described in section 5.7, the event history can be filtered by time, event type or number of events.

6.3.4 Subscription API

It seems to be only possible to configure subscriptions via webhook dashboard (see section 3.2.6), a subscription API does not seem to be offered, possibly for security reasons.

6.3.5 Non-Functional Properties

6.3.5.1 Security

Stripe offers a relatively high grade of security on its webhooks. The sender signs events using an HMAC-SHA256 algorithm. The resulting signature is transferred in the `Stripe-Signature` HTTP header. The shared secret for the signature is assigned by Stripe, not as in other solutions where the client gets to choose the secret. By producing the secret itself, Stripe can make sure that the secret has sufficient levels of entropy.

HTTPS is not enforced, but if a receiver endpoint with HTTPS protocol is configured, the certificates of the receiver endpoint are checked.

Stripe publishes the IP addresses of its event senders on the API portal, so clients can whitelist them.

6.3.5.2 Developer Experience

It seems to be only possible to configure subscriptions via a webhook dashboard, a subscription API does not seem to be offered. This limits the degree of automation.

Stripe offers good support for testing via the webhook dashboard. There is a dedicated mode for testing, which uses synthetic data and allows for sending test events.

6.4 BitBucket

BitBucket provides Git and Mercurial code management for professional development teams. Thanks to its REST APIs and webhooks, it is possible to integrate other applications with BitBucket.

A typical integration flow with BitBucket is: every time a developer pushes a commit in a repository, the continuous integration server should start a build. In this example, BitBucket delivers the event that initiates the integration workflow.

6.4.1 Events

Events are delivered as thick events via HTTP requests. The meta-data of the events is transported in the HTTP headers, leaving the HTTP body for transporting the resources which are affected by the event. The HTTP body contains the resources in a format comparable to an API response on the respective resource.

BitBucket offers a wide range of event types, which coincide with the typical operations of source code management software, such as push, fork, update etc. An overview of the available event types is provided on the API portal for human consumption and by the `/hook_events` endpoint for consumption by machines.

6.4.2 Subscription API

In BitBucket, subscriptions can be set up and managed via the webhook dashboard or the subscription API. The subscription API (called `/hooks` API in BitBucket) works as described in this book, but does not require a confirmation from the receiver endpoints. Bitbucket also offers the option to deactivate a subscription temporarily.

6.4.3 Non-Functional Properties

6.4.3.1 Security

When it comes to security, BitBucket webhooks provide an event signature (HMAC) based on a shared secret. BitBucket advocates that clients use HTTPS with official server certificates, but allow to switch certificate verification off to allow for self-signed certificates. IP addresses for whitelisting of the BitBucket event sender are provided. The API endpoints of Bitbucket, e.g. the subscription API, are protected by OAuth.

6.4.3.2 Reliability

When it comes to reliability, BitBucket does not tolerate failing webhook integrations for very long. Misbehaving or failing webhooks will be temporarily disabled. A timeout of 10 seconds is enforced for webhooks.

6.4.3.3 Developer Experience

BitBucket offers a sophisticated dashboard for managing webhooks and view the activity on the associated webhook endpoints in an event log. For each type of event, the event log shows the timestamp of the last success, the last failure, and the percentage of successful vs. unsuccessful calls to the webhook endpoints.

6.5 GitHub

GitHub is a development platform, which offers project management tools, code hosting and a social network of developers. With webhooks, clients can subscribe to events published by GitHub and build powerful integrations. For example, webhooks can be used to update an external issue tracker, trigger continuous integration builds, update a backup mirror, or even deploy to your production server.

Check out the GitHub webhooks tutorial
https://developer.github.com/webhooks
and the GitHub API reference documentation
https://developer.github.com/v3/repos/hooks

6.5.1 Events

GitHub uses thick events, so it delivers the affected resource alongside with the event. Each event type has a specific payload format with the relevant event information. GitHub knows a large number of event types and even offers a wildcard event that will match all supported events.

6.5.2 Event Receiver Endpoint

The number of receiver endpoints per event type and client is limited. Up to 20 receiver endpoints can be configured for each event type. Events can be delivered in either of two content types:

- The `application/json` content type delivers the JSON payload directly in the HTTP body.

- The `application/x-www-form-urlencoded` content type encodes the JSON payload in a form parameter called `payload`.

6.5.3 Event History API

GitHub offers a read-only event history API (called `/events` endpoint) to keep track of the history of events and for manual reconciliation after events have been missed. The API is split up into several endpoints. Each major resource in GitHub, such as `repositories`, `networks`, and `orgs`, offer a separate events endpoint as a subresource.

6.5.4 Subscription API

The subscription API is mounted deep in the URL structure of GitHub, and it is called `/hooks`. It is actually realized as a subresource of the `/repos/{owner-id}/{rep-id}` resource.

The URL structure makes clear, which resource the subscription applies to.

There is no confirmation logic for new subscriptions. Instead, GitHub offers a ping endpoint as part of each subscription on `/repos/{owner-id}/{rep-id}/hooks/{hook-id}/ping`. It sends a ping event to the receiver. GitHub also offers a test endpoint on `/repos/{owner-id}/{rep-id}hooks/{hook-id}/test` as part of each individual subscription. When called, the test endpoint (re-)sends the latest push event to the receiver.

Besides the JSON API described above, GitHub also offers an alternative API for managing webhooks based on WebSub and PubSubHubbub (see section 2.6).

6.5.5 Non-Functional Properties

6.5.5.1 Security

GitHub offers message signatures, which are transferred in the `X-Hub-Signature` HTTP header. The shared secret is created on the client side.

6.5.5.2 Developer Experience

On its API portal, GitHub offers next to the obligatory documentation and tutorials, a webhook dashboard with functionality to register webhooks and view recent events. This event viewer is quite extensive and allows us to inspect the request and response of each event delivery, including HTTP headers and HTTP body.

7 Developing Webhook Endpoints

Developing webhook endpoints is a lot like developing any RESTful endpoint or API, so it is essential to have a good understanding of APIs and REST [4].

But unlike APIs, webhooks are not supposed to be called directly by various API clients. Instead, they are only called by the event sender, and unless they interoperate with the event sender, they are useless. It is thus difficult to create a realistic testing setup. To deal with this special situation and allow for independent development and testing in a controlled environment, we propose the following practical stepping stones and tools for developing webhooks:

1. Inspect the events that are sent from the API provider (see section 7.1).

2. Generate real and artificial events using the webhook dashboard (see section 3.2.6) or ping endpoint (see section 7.2).

3. Create a mock sender, which allows creating all the events needed to test the webhooks implementation (see section 7.3).

4. Develop and test the webhook endpoint locally, using artificial events from the mock server and then some real events from the API provider (see section 7.4).

5. Deploy the webhook endpoint on an environment that satisfies the non-functional requirements of webhook receivers (see section 7.5).

7.1 Inspect Events

Before building a webhook endpoint, consumers may want to inspect the events produced by the API provider. They need to see what kind of events arrive on their end and what the requests and payloads look like.

RequestBin (https://requestb.in) is a tool that allows us to inspect the events sent by the API provider. RequestBin allows us to generate a unique URL and collect the requests made to it. These requests are recorded and stored in a database. We can then log into the RequestBin web UI to inspect the recorded requests in a human-friendly way.

To set up RequestBin, we create a new URL and subscribe to an event with the RequestBin URL as receiver endpoint. To inspect events with this setup, we need to create some events. Events can be produced by interacting live with the API provider to make it naturally produce an event. Alternatively, artificial test events or ping events can be generated via the webhook dashboard (see section 3.2.6) or API (see section 7.2), whatever the API provider offers.

7.2 Generate Events

API providers should offer the possibility to generate a ping event or test event for a specific webhook. Sometimes this functionality is offered on the webhook dashboard (see section 3.2.6) or as an API endpoint. An example is the ping endpoint: When the ping endpoint is called, it generates a synthetic event for testing and sends it off to the webhook. In our webhook design proposal, we have integrated such a ping endpoint as a part of the subscription API (see section 5.5.3.2). One of the advantages of providing test events via API is that they can be used for automated integration testing.

7.3 Mock the Event Sender

Once the events have been understood, due to event inspection (see section 7.1) of generated and real data, we build a repeatable test suite. For this reason, one can set up a mock sender which can generate and send all kinds of events to the webhook endpoint we want to test. A simple way of building a mock server is using Postman (https://www.getpostman.com) or SOAP-UI (https://www.soapui.org).

7.4 Develop the Event Receiver

Typically, developers want to implement, debug and test the receiver locally in a development environment. If we want to test it locally, we can only test it with the artificial events produced by the mock server (see section 7.3). What to do when we want to test the receiver against some real events from the API provider? To be able to receive real events from the API provider, the receiver needs to be accessible from the public internet. The developer machine, however, should not be accessible from the internet.

Ngrok (https://ngrok.com) is a tool that exposes local servers behind NATs and firewalls to the public internet via a secure tunnel. Ngrok consists of two components: A cloud component and a local component that needs to be installed on the local machine. Between the two components, Ngrok establishes a secure tunnel. The Ngrok cloud component provides a publicly accessible URL. Whatever is sent to that public URL is tunneled to the local installation of Ngrok and made available to the local development server. This setup allows us to make our event receiver endpoint available on the internet and accessible for the event sender, even though it is running on a local development machine.

To set this system up, we need to create an event subscription with the Ngrok URL as the receiver. Now the events arrive from the API provider on our local receiver, where we can test and debug the receiver based on real event data.

Even though this setup is working for development, we need to deploy the receiver for production (see section 7.5).

7.5 Deploy the Event Receiver

The receiver can be deployed on any application server that can fulfill the requirements of the event receiver regarding security, reliability, and availability. Receivers need to be highly available, able to deal with high load and not miss an event. Scaling and elasticity are important. Ideally, receivers support HTTPS and use a certificate that is signed by a trusted authority.

These features are quite tall demands for a small web service endpoint. But all these requirements can also be satisfied by a serverless infrastructure out of the cloud. Such a serverless infrastructure is offered by all major cloud providers. So when deploying a receiver, we should consider if it makes sense to deploy the receiver on a serverless infrastructure in the cloud.

Appendix

Feedback

If you enjoyed this book and got some value from it, it would be great if you could share with others what you liked about the book on the Amazon review page.

If you feel something was missing or you are not satisfied with your purchase, please contact me at matt@api-university.com. I read this email personally and am very interested in your feedback.

About the Author

Matthias has provided expertise to international and national companies on software architecture, software development processes, and software integration. At some point, he got a PhD.

Nowadays, Matthias uses his background in software engineering to help companies to realize their digital transformation agenda and to bring innovative software solutions to the market.

He also loves sharing his knowledge in the classroom, at workshops, and in his books. Matthias is an instructor at the API-University, publishes a blog on APIs, is the author of several books on APIs and regularly speaks at technology conferences.

Other Products by the Author

Book on RESTful API Design

Looking for Best Practices in RESTful APIs?

This book is for you! Why? Because this book is packed with best practices on many technical aspects of RESTful API Design, such as the correct use of resources, URIs, representations, content types, data formats, parameters, HTTP status codes and HTTP methods.

You want to design and develop APIs like a Pro? Use API description languages to both design APIs and develop APIs efficiently. The book introduces the two most common API description languages RAML and OpenAPI/Swagger.

Your APIs connect to legacy systems? The book shows best practices for connecting APIs to existing backend systems.

You expect lots of traffic on your API? The book shows you how to achieve high security, performance, availability and smooth evolution and versioning.

Your company cares about its customers? Learn a customer-centric design and development approach for APIs, so you can design APIs as digital products.

Title: RESTful API Design
Author: Matthias Biehl
Release Date: 2016-08-30
Length: 290 pages
ISBN-13: 978-1514735169

https://api-university.com/books/api-design

Book on GraphQL API Design

Want to build APIs like Facebook? Since Facebook's framework for building APIs, GraphQL, has become publicly available, this ambition seems to be within reach for many companies. And that is great. But first, let's learn what GraphQL really is and – maybe even more importantly – let's figure out how to apply GraphQL to build APIs that consumers love.

In this book, we take a hands-on approach to learning GraphQL. We first explore the concepts of the two GraphQL languages using examples. Then we start writing some code for our first GraphQL API. We develop this API step by step, from creating a schema and resolving queries, over mocking data and connecting data sources all the way to developing mutations and setting up event subscriptions.

Are your API consumers important to you? This book shows you how to apply a consumer-oriented design process for GraphQL APIs.

Do you want to enable the API consumers so they can build great apps? This book explains the GraphQL query language, which allows the API consumers to retrieve data, write data and get notified when data changes.

Do you want to make your API easy and intuitive to use? This book shows you how to use the GraphQL schema language to define a type system for your API.

Title: GraphQL API Design
Author: Matthias Biehl
Release Date: 2018-01-30
Length: 90 pages
ISBN-13: 978-1979717526

https://api-university.com/books/graphql-api-design

Book on API Architecture

Looking for the big picture of building APIs? This book is for you!

Building APIs that consumers love should certainly be the goal of any API initiative. However, it is easier said than done. It requires getting the architecture for your APIs right. This book equips you with both foundations and best practices for API architecture. This book presents best practices for putting an infrastructure in place that enables efficient development of APIs. This book is for you if you want to understand the big picture of API design and development, you want to define an API architecture, establish a platform for APIs or simply want to build APIs your consumers love. What is API architecture? Architecture spans the bigger picture of APIs and can be seen from several perspectives: The architecture of the complete solution, the technical architecture of the API platform, the architecture of the API portfolio, the design decisions for a particular API proxy. This book covers all of the above perspectives on API architecture. However, to become useful, the architecture needs to be put into practice. This is why this book covers an API methodology for design and development. An API methodology provides practical guidelines for putting API architecture into practice. It explains how to develop an API architecture into an API that consumers love.

Title: API Architecture
Author: Matthias Biehl
Release Date: 2015-05-22
Length: 190 pages
ISBN-13: 978-1508676645

https://api-university.com/books/api-architecture

Book on OpenID Connect

What is the difference between OAuth 2 and OpenID Connect?

For API security there are two standards — and they both start with O. So it is no wonder, people ask all the time what the difference between the two is.

If you have read the OAuth 2 Book, you already know a lot about OAuth. The OAuth standard ensures that there is no unintended leakage of information about the resource owner to the client. For example, it is ensured that the client does not get hold of the resource owner's credentials. The OAuth standard ensures the privacy of the resource owner. However, there are cases, where the client should have the possibility to get access to specific profile information of the resource owner.

Title: OpenID Connect - Identity Layer for your API

Author: Matthias Biehl

Release Date: 2018-02-28

Length: 90 pages

ISBN-13: 978-1979718479

https://api-university.com/books/openid-connect

Book on OAuth 2.0

This book offers an introduction to API Security with OAuth 2.0. In less than 80 pages you will gain an overview of the capabilities of OAuth. You will learn the core concepts of OAuth. You will get to know all 4 OAuth Flows that are used for cloud solutions and mobile apps. If you have tried to read the official OAuth specification, you may get the impression that OAuth is complicated. This book explains OAuth in simple terms. The different OAuth Flows are visualized graphically using sequence diagrams. The diagrams allow you to see the big picture of the various OAuth interactions. This high-level overview is complemented with a rich set of example requests and responses and an explanation of the technical details. In the book, the challenges and benefits of OAuth are presented, followed by an explanation of the technical concepts of OAuth. The technical concepts include the actors, endpoints, tokens and the four OAuth flows. Each flow is described in detail, including the use cases for each flow. Extensions of OAuth - so-called profiles - are presented, such as OpenID Connect and the SAML2 Bearer Profile. Sequence diagrams are presented to explain the necessary interactions.

Title: OAuth 2.0 - Getting Started in Web-API Security
Author: Matthias Biehl
Release Date: 2014-11-15
Length: 76 pages
ISBN-13: 978-1507800911

https://api-university.com/books/oauth-2-0-book

122

Online Course on OAuth 2.0

Securing APIs is complicated? This course offers an introduction to API Security with OAuth 2.0. In 3 hours you will gain an overview of the capabilities of OAuth. You will learn the core concepts of OAuth. You will get to know all 4 OAuth flows that are used for cloud solutions and mobile apps. You will also be able to look over the shoulder of an expert using OAuth for the APIs of Facebook, LinkedIn, Google and Paypal.

Title: OAuth 2.0 - Getting Started in Web-API Security

Lecturer: Matthias Biehl

Release Date: 2015-07-30

Material: Video, Workbooks, Quizzes

Length: 4h

https://api-university.com/courses/oauth-2-0-course

Online Course on RESTful API Design

Looking for best practices of RESTful API Design? This course is for you! Why? This course provides interactive video tutorials on the best practices of RESTful design. These best practices are based on the lessons learned from building and designing APIs over many years.

The course also includes video lectures on technical aspects of RESTful API Design, including the correct use of resources, URIs, representations, content-types, data formats, parameters, HTTP status codes and HTTP methods. And thanks to many interactive quizzes, learning REST becomes an engaging and exciting game-like experience.

We focus on the practical application of the knowledge, to get you ready for your first RESTful API project. The course includes guided mini-projects to get you ready for the practical application of REST.

After completing this course, you will be able to design RESTful APIs – but not just any APIs, you have all the knowledge to design APIs, which your consumers will love.

Title: RESTful API Design

Lecturer: Matthias Biehl

Release Date: 2018-01-01

Material: Video, Workbooks, Quizzes

Length: 3h

https://api-university.com/courses/restful-api-design-course

124

Bibliography

[1] The WebSocket API. Technical report, W3C, September 2012. 2.5

[2] Server-Sent events. Technical report, W3C, February 2015. 2.4

[3] Matthias Biehl. *OAuth 2.0: Getting Started in Web-API Security (API University Series) (Volume 1)*. CreateSpace Independent Publishing Platform, 1 edition, January 2015. 4.2.3, 6.2.6.1

[4] Matthias Biehl. *RESTful API Design: Best Practices in API Design with REST (API-University Series Book 3)*. 1 edition, August 2016. 5.1, 7

[5] Linux Foundation. OpenAPI specification 3.0. Technical report, Linux Foundation, July 2017. 1.4, 4.4.2, 5.1

[6] Julien Genestoux, Brad Fitzpatrick, Brett Slatkin, and Martin Atkins. WebSub. Technical report, W3C, October 2017. 2.6

[7] Dick Hardt. The OAuth 2.0 authorization framework. Technical Report 6749, RFC Editor, Fremont, CA, USA, October 2012. 4.2.3, 4.2.4, 5.5.3.2, 6.2.6.1

[8] Mark Nottingham. Web linking. Technical Report 5988, RFC Editor, Fremont, CA, USA, October 2010. 2.6

[9] E. Rescorla. HTTP over TLS. Technical Report 2818, RFC Editor, Fremont, CA, USA, May 2000. 4.2.2.3, 4.2.3, 4.2.4

Index

Printed in Great Britain
by Amazon